CORPORATE BUSINESS DESIGN

Armadillo Publishers. Melbourne.

ACN 005649712

Administration and co-ordination by Elaine Howell.
Design concept & art direction by David Lyons.

Published & produced in Australia
by Armadillo Publishers Pty Ltd,
205-207 Scotchmer Street, Fitzroy North,
Victoria 3068 Australia.
(03) 489 9559 Fax. (03) 489 5576.

Special thanks to:
Jennifer Richardson.
Dianne Gameson.
Rick Altman.
Chia Pee Teck.
Desmond Heng.

Printed and bound in Singapore by Imago Productions.
Typesetting by The Composing Room, Melbourne.

 ISSN 1035-9222.

CORPORATE BUSINESS DESIGN

PHOTOGRAPHY

DESIGN

CORPORATE CONSULTANTS

ANNUAL REPORT REPORT

GREEN PAGES

In today's highly competitive and somewhat frenetic world of commerce, the manner in which a Company is perceived becomes more and more crucial.

Whilst the promotion and advertising of a Company's product is the top priority, it is becoming increasingly vital to portray the actual company in a positive light also.

Should a company wish to obtain extra financing, to raise a share float, acquire a new partner, market itself for sale, or present its credentials for some other purpose, the promotional material it has in hand or is able to quickly produce, can enormously influence its success in these times.

Annual reports and financial statements, promotional documents, historical chronicles, newsletters, executive profiles, even internal dossiers and memoranda, will all benefit from sensitive, communicative design and quality presentation.

For all the companies which are already aware of the need for good communicating tools, there are just as many who would do well to take stock and call for the experts.

In this, the inaugural edition of Corporate Business Design we show you work by some of Australia's leading exponents in the field of corporate photography, design and communication. People who will understand your requirements and ensure you achieve your communication goals.

You'll find samples of their work, some which is immediately recognisable, and which will lead you to its creators should you like the style. However, we are also pleased to be able to present work which has had very little public exposure due to its very nature, and this is one of the benefits of such a publication. Seeing such a diversity of work can help you formulate your requirements and tastes.

Whilst this first edition is not large, we believe we have created an entity from which future editions can expand.

We trust you will discover the creativity and expertise you are seeking within its pages.

Elaine Howell & David Lyons.
Armadillo Publishers

THE EMPEROR'S CLOTHES.

Corporate graphic artists have long understood that design is a powerful management tool. Not every corporate leader would accept this, even in consumer-orientated industries.

Competition for readers' attention is fierce. About 90 per cent of shareholders spend five minutes or less scanning an annual report. Good design can make important corporate literature, such as the report, accessible for a wider range of people and can help to focus the communication better on specific, important audiences.

Over the past two decades, graphic artists in Australia have risen to the challenge of corporate design as effectively as anywhere in the world. Our artists are especially strong in the practical aspects of corporate design. They make the effort to understand their clients' operations as well as the technical challenges of implementing design in such areas as corporate identity and product development.

Graphic designers can help clients to project a better image probably than the clients merit. But, also, there is some truth in the old adage that while editors (and corporate communicators) can't visualise, designers don't read. There is a wealth of information, including reasonably up-to-date Australian research, about how best to lay out type to attract the reader, and to make the message easier to read and remember. Unfortunately some graphic artists don't give type the importance it deserves, regarding it as just another graphic element.

Publication design can require a different approach, even different skills, than other forms of corporate design including identity design, promotional or advertising design, or product design and literature.

The need for effective corporate communications, including annual reports and capability brochures, has never been greater. Business has to look to getting the most value from each design project.

Annual reports, corporate brochures and journals are vitally important, being among the few communication links between the chief executive and critically important external and internal audiences. Good corporate designers are sensitive to the need to help communicate finely honed strategic messages and information for investment analysts, stockbrokers and financial journalists as well as shareholders, and line management and other employees.

Not all business communicators have the experience, the time or the aptitude to accurately and confidently assess the contribution of the design component in important messages and depend, correctly, on professional advice from their design consultants. But consultants have been known to be guilty of the *Emperor's Clothes* syndrome: 'Because I say it is so, it is so'. Sadly the result can be a communication which, though visually appealing, is poorly conceived and ineffectual. Design for its own sake will get in the way of communicating the message.

Good design will effectively project an organisation's style and substance, showing that it knows what it is doing and where it is going, enhancing the corporation's credibility in its markets and among investors, and helping sustain employee motivation.

The good news is that Australian corporations are generally well served by graphic designers who understand the importance of being aware of the needs of their clients.

After years of observing the breed, I have noted some phrases which any aspiring corporate graphic artist should find useful:

There's no need to shout. Use this to assuage the wounded sensitivities of clients who know they don't have a good story to tell.

Never show an idiot half a story. This is a piece of advice (somewhat akin to advice about not giving suckers an even break) to remind the designer not to show a client a design rough. I firmly disagree, but then I may have been the person in question.

You shouldn't be a slave to form. This handy little phrase can be used, for example, when an error has been found in a job which has already been printed several thousand times and you feel a need to justify not reprinting.

Intelligent flexibility. My favourite. Clients use this expression when they want to change something, or to try to confuse the graphic designer – it never works. Graphic artists must be taught in college to ignore this ploy.

Douglas Davidson
Manager corporate affairs
CSR Limited

A CHANGE FOR THE BETTER?

When a corporation is suffering from a downturn in profits, sees a bad trading period ahead, or wishes to be perceived in a different light than it currently is, an identity crisis can result.

Can change be affected with the company's visual I.D. as it currently appears?

An astute company looks logically at all angles of its operation, firstly from inside, and then it may call in outside experts as well.

Finally proposed changes are weighed up, discussed, discarded or recommended. It could be found that it's necessary to vary staff training procedures, new financial and accounting arrangements, sometimes a total re-structuring programme is undertaken.

However, the thing that makes the biggest initial impact in the marketplace is a new look – a new corporate visual image.

It could start with the reworking of a well known logo to bring it into the current era. Sometimes these changes are so subtle they're not even obvious unless pointed out. In this way many world famous images have kept pace with progress for the last 50 plus years.

However, in most cases, there's a decided swing towards sweeping out everything that currently exists and starting afresh.

This can be very dangerous, but generally comes down to how well known and how well received the current logo is, and how well known and how well perceived the company currently is.

If a new broom is needed, so be it.

Choose a designer/consultant you've never worked with before – but one whose work you admire. If it's more of a re-vamp on an existing logo, it's generally wiser and more successful to stay with (if possible the one who designed your original logo) who should be delighted to enhance their initial design.

The logo is the germ from which all other elements of the corporate image stem. If you don't see it as the company's all-embracing image, get rid of it. A logo is usually carried through on every piece of company communication – whether it's product, stationery, signage, vehicular, and in some cases on clothing too.

Obviously the CEO has to be happy with it. However, it is going to work even better if the company executives and staff are also happy with it, as they'll proudly display it at every opportunity and carry through its communicating message. Naturally people who work in advertising and design areas are far more critical to a company's image than the public who are not so concerned. But it is surprising how positive or negative these images can become to the public when they are featured in a new story on television or at a big sporting event.

It's been stated by some of the world's leading corporate image designers that it's difficult to assess whether the cost of a change to a logo is justified in terms of return for dollars outlaid.

In large organisations the changeover cost after a design is approved can reach phenomenal heights. In many cases the change has been necessary – perhaps to reflect a change in ownership, or the incorporation of a new companies into a group, etc. But when a logo is designed purely to enhance the company's image, and where no other real changes are being made, then research into the success of a new logo is sometimes difficult to ascertain.

However, if you compare the cost of a new company image via a new logo, and thus the follow-through of all identifying company accoutrements, with paid media such as the press and electronic media, then if the logo is right, the cost can be shown to be top value.

What to keep in mind when the design of a new logo is put forward:

Do we really need it?

Will it change our company's perception of ourselves?

Will it change our clients perception of our company?

Will it encourage new clients/ customers?

Or will it carry us through to the future?

Will it help us?

AUSTRALIA FARE.

It is sometimes claimed that Australia is a most desirable country, spoiled only by the apathy of its people. This apathy is explained as being the direct result of our temperate climate and abundant natural resources. In contrast, the theory goes, people from colder climates are more industrious and perhaps more inventive.

This may or may not be true but the great irony of our country is that Australians, particularly original and creative Australians, do suffer considerable adversity in order to succeed in their chosen fields. The barriers to achievement exist in our everyday lives and are so entrenched in our psyche that they have labels... "Cultural Cringe", "Tall Poppy Syndrome", not "International" and so on.

We are our own harshest critics. We relentlessly substitute human criticism and adversity for the lack of hardship imposed by Nature. And it is far more insidious for it can undermine the desire for originality, the drive to be different, to be Australian.

That is why books like "The Wizards of Oz" and this new book, CBD are so important for our well-being. In their pages are many examples of successful Australian creative output judged in the most severe way possible – by the ringing of a cash register.

This creativity may be said to be a little unsophisticated when judged by "International" standards (whatever that means!) But our alleged "unsophistication" is our strength. Australian creativity is at once... young, fresh, vital and original. It is unique. And that, ultimately, is what a client seeks from a creative brief.

The essential Australian creativity is not like anything out of London, New York or Rome. Let's capitalise on this as some of the smarter Australians have – Ken Done,"Crocodile Dundee", Dame Edna and many Australian winemakers have all succeeded by being Australian. Let's think of exporting the results of our singular talents. They are eminently marketable.

Let us recognise that to do this we have to actively resist the natural environment that makes life so easy here. This environment that gives us the world's cheapest wheat, fine wool, coal, milk and numerous other primary products is deceiving us into not applying our skills to add unique value to our natural assets.

The combination of these cheap raw materials from Nature and the intrinsic "Cultural Cringe" from ourselves is inhibiting us from being one of the great creative nations of the world.

Let us add our special value to everything we are lucky enough to possess.

Let's use our abundant sunlight for brilliant photography and film making.

Let's paint the ochres, the burnt siennas, the cobalt blues of the Australian landscape.

Let's make use of our unique animals as symbols for our successful corporations (it works for Qantas).

Let's capitalise, on all our creativity, on the fundamental friendliness, informality and easy-going nature of the Australian.

Let us do the one thing that Australians do better than any culture – let's improvise. Let's create from what we have on hand, not from what we can borrow from overseas.

Tony Hollway.
Export Director, Kraft Foods.

ART VERSUS DESIGN.

Graphic Design is not art. It has purpose. Art and design are as different to one another as poetry and journalism.

Australia has a unique opportunity of not being driven by graphic design styles of the northern hemisphere.

Australian design will become important when marketers accept its potency and designers accept client resistance.

Only then will graphic design have a firm position in the marketplace.

Ronny Ruhlmann.
Crackerjack Design Group.
Sydney.

INTRODUCING AGDA:
THE AUSTRALIAN GRAPHIC DESIGN ASSOCIATION.

The Australian Graphic Design Association was formed in 1988 with a dedication to address a number of industry problems and to set industry standards which would become the hallmarks of the professional designer.

Since its formation AGDA has dramatically altered the outlook of the design profession. A program of seminars. debates, social events, educational activities and workshops has created opportunities for many people to meet, to learn new skills, and to exchange ideas and information.

A constitution has been incorporated to establish a philosophical framework as well as an organisational structure based on a network of councils throughout Australia co-ordinated by a national council.

AGDA is able to operate successfully because it is supported by its members who pay annual membership fees as well as supplying the energy and ideas necessary to run the organisation. Elected state councils develop local programs and initiatives which are implemented by project committees and also a number of committed and energetic members.

Over the long term, members will benefit from the guidelines AGDA is setting for training, professional practice, codes of conduct, contracts and a resource for industrial arbitration. Over the short term, AGDA will continue to offer its members the opportunity to participate in its events (with concession rates); purchase books at discounted prices; and receive AGDA guidelines and technical papers free of charge.

Membership of the organisation is open to anyone involved in or associated with the graphic design industry. This includes illustrators, designers, art directors, writers and photographers as well as manufacturers and suppliers of products and services to the graphic arts industry.

While the Association is run principally by designers for designers, AGDA is an organisation which believes that designers' interests are best served by considering the position of all contingent interests in the industry. Consequently categories of membership are designed to accommodate industry-wide participation.

Upon joining the organisation a member may become involved on another level by serving on one of a series of committees (such as education, social events, recruitment, etc.) or by being elected to either the state or national councils of the organisation.

AGDA would like to encourage all design practitioners and relevant associated individuals or organisations to join and participate in the Association for their own interests, for the long term benefit of the Association and also, to ensure the continuing profile of Australia's design industry both nationally and internationally.
For further details telephone (03) 429 9892.

Wayne Rankin,
President. Melbourne.

SEND IT OUT.

What do garbage collection, legal advice, graphic design, and computer operations have in common?

Each represents an example of how corporations are achieving significant strategic advantage or cost savings through the implementation of 'outsourcing'. To the uninitiated, 'outsourcing' is the complete turning over or sharing of responsibility for all or part of a service/function to a third party. In essence, it means that it can often be cheaper and more effective to not do things inhouse but to delegate specific tasks to individuals/groups outside the organisation whose distinctive competence is in that field.

Example. It has traditionally been accepted that organisations of any reasonable size should buy and run their own computer centres and in so doing, were required to invest heavily in procuring the resources to operate effectively.

Despite the fact that the organisation's core business may have been gold mining, retailing, manufacturing or banking, it wasn't questioned whether operating it from within, was the most prudent thing to do. There didn't appear to be any credible alternatives anyway and the mystique which the world of technology had created, successfully undermined the confidence of most executives in challenging the status quo.

As a result and as organisations became

more dependent on the quality of their information systems through the 60s, 70s and early 80s, we saw the high injection of funding into the establishment of larger, inhouse computer departments.

Whilst there were and are many success stories, others have now started to question whether there might be a better way – whether they could even save money, and at the same time allow themselves to focus again on their own raison d'etre – perhaps widget making or flying planes. How? By identifying suitable partners, external to their business, whose very specialisation is information technology and who could therefore deliver more effective results.

If we look at recent trends, it would appear that the incidence of 'outsourcing' is growing steadily and the success exemplified by many of the 'early adopters' would suggest that the concept warrants at least serious consideration.

The same principle which applies to the procurement of specialist skills in computing, applies in other specialist areas, and in particular reference to this publication, that of visual design/ photography.

The organisations shown here represent the experts in their respective industries, and as this book testifies, their specialisation has given them the experience and knowledge of techniques necessary to produce the best results.

Just as organisations are recognising the contribution which information technology can make to their ultimate success, so are they now recognising the immense value and strategic advantage which can be gained through the creativity and skill inherent in good advertising and effective publicity.

Today's competitive pressures demand that we strive always to create the best – to erase mediocrity – and given that employees can't be experts in all the tasks required of them, perhaps there is a justification for the application of 'outsourcing' in the field of visual design. The question as to whether a particular set of tasks requires the use of an expert can only be answered by judging the potential difference in results.

Rosemary Tilley.
Consulting Principal,
DMR Group Australia.

PHOTOGRAPHY.

Principally, I'm a location photographer. By land, sea or air, I go wherever you need a shot taken. I'm happy to work solo, with just one assistant, or with the whole box and dice of a travelling production team.

Naturally I love to have strong ideas to work to, but where the idea is not formulated prior to the shoot, I enjoy the challenge of reaching out for the best in every situation and grabbing the vital elements, enhancing the natural attributes, thriving in all kinds of light and circumstances.

Creating mobile light sources within the confines of industrial locations is another characteristic of my work.

Being a top technician is one thing. Being able to think on your feet and take complete advantage of any situation is another.

Split second timing, being able to handle the equipment as quickly as I'm formulating the frame, can catch the once-in-a-lifetime moment, and add a unique aspect to a series.

Whether it's out the back of Bourke, in the city, within manufacturing plants, factories or offices, or on sumptuous assignments throughout the world – I'll willingly go almost anywhere you choose to send me.

I love being on location, to begin looking for an inventive approach to best illustrate your product or service.

When I'm shooting, my back-up at The Lighthouse ensures you have ease of contact and follow-through on every phase of the job.

I'll continue to look for a clean, graphic, approach to shooting each location, and look forward to capturing the perfect image for you and posterity.

JOHN HOLLAND.
VICTORIAN TOURIST COMMISSION.
LAMINEX INDUSTRIES.

V I T T O R I O

JOHN HOLLAND.
CATO DESIGN.

L O C A T I O N

JOE VITTORIO. THE LIGHTHOUSE. 5 LITTLE CHAPEL STREET, PRAHRAN, VICTORIA
3181 AUSTRALIA. TELEPHONE (03) 529 2144. FAX: 529 6953. PAGER: 883 5247

ASPECT PHOTOGRAPHICS

As owner of Aspect Photographics, I have built my business over the last 12 years providing consistently good photography and service.

At Aspect, we specialise in photography for Annual Reports, Corporate Brochures and Industrial applications. With 23 years of experience, my forte is location work . . . producing excellent ground or aerial shots.

A professional team combined with impressive, well equipped studios enables us to satisfy any photographic need. Our main studio features a 17 metre long cyclorama, the latest in German lighting technology, a floodable floor, large rear roller door access and a shooting board for taking overhead pictures. Our portrait studio is permanently set up with its own lighting and photographic equipment taking the time factor out of portrait photography. Busy executives are on their way in a matter of minutes and due to the permanent nature of the studio, the results are always excellent.

Our E6 colour processing facility ensures product confidentiality, quick turn-around time and, like all of our services is competitively priced.

I believe we offer one of the most professional photographic services in Adelaide.

K E V I N   O ' D A L Y

ASPECT PHOTOGRAPHICS PTY LTD

177 HALIFAX ST ADELAIDE SOUTH AUSTRALIA

FACSIMILE (08) 232 1260 TELEPHONE (08) 224 0113

IF YOUR COMPANY IS PROUD OF IT'S IMAGE, CONSULT A PROUD IMAGE MAKER.

Marketing a company's image is as important as marketing the commodities, or services that it offers. A qaulity facade is indicative of a company with pride, and the hallmark of a company that cares.

When considering photographic illustration for your annual report, corporate brochure or prospectus, it is equally important to select the skills of a photographer with experience in this exacting field, one who understands the importance of 'the company image'.

Melbourne based illustrative photographer Rick Altman can draw on twenty years of experience photographing for high profile Australian Corporations.

Self employed since 1972, Rick has travelled extensively throughout Australia on assignments for major mining, industrial and manufacturing organisations, bringing far away outposts into the boardrooms of the major cities through his images. He approaches his assignments with thorough research into the company, strengthening his ability to produce creative images, imaginative and personalised presentations specific for the needs of the client.

The broad spectrum of his portfolio highlights the esteem with which this skilled photographer is held. A major petroleum refinery in Queensland, computer equipment manufacturing at a Melbourne based hi-tech company, mining black gold for world export, steel reinforcing on a Melbourne building site, are but a few of the diverse projects he has successfully completed.

Conscious of the clients' needs, he is highly professional in his dealings with them. Insisting on a thorough briefing and gathering of background information prior to undertaking an assignment for his clients. On completion, a first class presentation of photography is made. Rick believes these are integral to the success of high acheivement. Busy companies do not have time to waste, nor does a busy photographer.

When a quality corporate print production to share holders, clients or consumers is required, and deadlines are to be met, precision and quality work are paramount. Rick Altman has collaborated with many prestigious design houses in producing quality corporate publications, his creative skills are in contant demand.

Over the past five years, Rick Altman has carried out photographic assignments for a wide range of companies including ACI International, the Albury/Wodonga Development Corporation, Alcatel-STC. Amcor, Australia Post, the Australian Wheat Board, the Australian Wool Corporation, BHP, Boral, BP Australia, Calgene Pacific, Caltex Australia, Coles Myer, Comalco, Commercial Polymers, CRA, Datacraft, Dow Chemicals, First Abbott Corporation, GMH, Jennings Industries, LM Ericsson, Mercedes-Benz (Australia), Metal Manufactures, Mobil Australia, Newmont Mining, Pacific Dunlop, Pilkington ACI, Price Waterhouse, Rover Holdings, Sigma, Telecom Australia, Tricom, Union Fidelity Trustee Company and Wesley College.

RICK ALTMAN ILLUSTRATIVE PHOTOGRAPHER MELBOURNE AUSTRALIA

RICK ALTMAN
ILLUSTRATIVE PHOTOGRAPHER
MELBOURNE AUSTRALIA

TELEPHONE 057 832045
PAGER 016 374822
FACSIMILE 057 832051

*Stock**shots***

Photographic Library
Oz Tourism
Agriculture
Industry/Mining
International Travel
People of all Nations
Sports & Leisure
Landscapes
Cityscapes

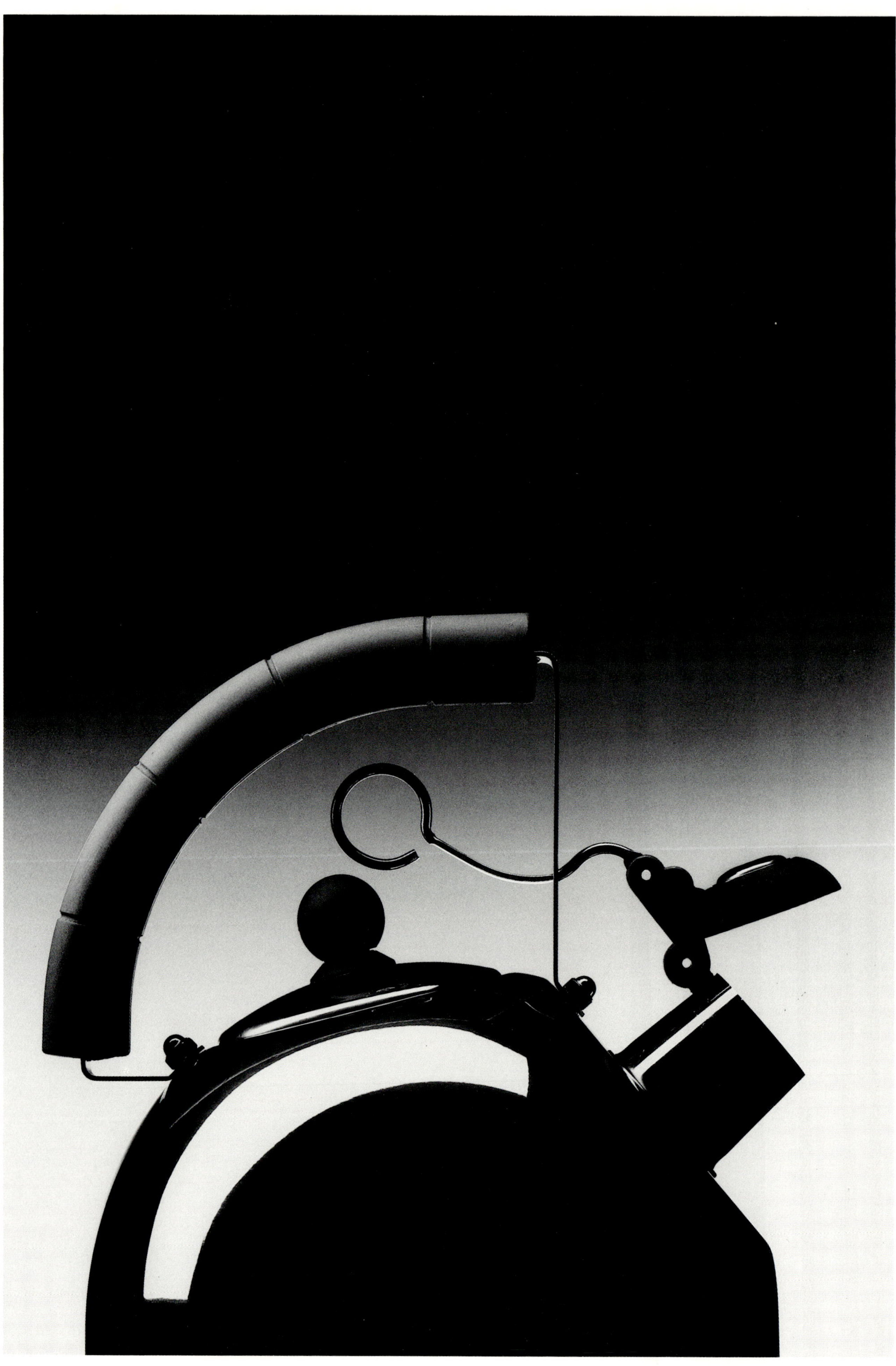

LLEWELLYNN

Mark Llewellynn

Photographer

2 Queens Place

Balmain NSW 2041

Tel (02) 810 2601

Fax (02) 555 1019

Bestobell

Caltex

CIG

Custom Credit

Dalgety

DEC

Digital

Friends Provident

Honeywell

NCR

Ogilvy and Mather

PEC

Sanwa Bank

Security Pacific

Young and Rubicam

Armitage Johannsen Architects

Australian Construction Service

Barclay Mowlem Construction

Burson-Marsteller

Carringbush

Civil & Civic

Coles Myer

Done Art & Design

Financial & Corporate Relations

Good Weekend Magazine

Grillglen Interior Designers

Havens Kirkwood & Meertens

Issues Australia

Jennings Industries

KPMG Peat Marwick

Lend Lease Interiors

Master Builders Association

Multiplex Constructions

Peddle Thorp & Walker

Reed Constructions

Revlon Australia

Whiteworks Public Relations

During the past six years, Fretwell Photography has enjoyed a steadily growing reputation for providing a creative and reliable service for an extensive and varied list of clients.

In an industry known for superficiality, you will find brothers Robert and Anthony personable, down to earth and very experienced.

Whilst the focus is on two key fields, corporate and architectural, Fretwell Photography are also commissioned for fashion and product work as well as fine art reproduction.

Fretwell Photography are official photographers for BOMA (Building Owners and Managers Association of Australia) Magazine and Good Weekend Magazine commissions a general service on a freelance basis.

" We offer a personal commitment to our work, combined with a reliable service. We take care to listen to our client's brief and work creatively within that brief (and budget). Our commitment to photography is great rather than simply good."

f

CLIENT: PRO-IMAGE PTY LTD. DESIGNER: AMANDA ROACH.

SIXTEEN ENTHUSIASTIC YEARS EXPERIENCE IN ADVERTISING, CORPORATE AND TRAVEL PHOT

LOOKING GOOD IN PRINT. PETER WALTON UNDERTAKES LOCAL, INTERSTATE AND OVERSEAS A

FOLIO AVAILABLE BY OVERNIGHT COURIER. A FLEXIBLE APPROACH T

CLIENT: NEWMONT AUSTRALIA LIMITED. DESIGNER: HANS BAUER.

PHY HAVE DEVELOPED A VALUABLE INSIGHT INTO THE IMPORTANT BUSINESS OF

CLIENT: BASF AUSTRALIA LIMITED. DESIGNER: MALCOMB SHEFFIELD.

NMENTS FOR A WIDE RANGE OF CLIENTS. FURTHER EXAMPLES ON THE NEXT TWO PAGES.

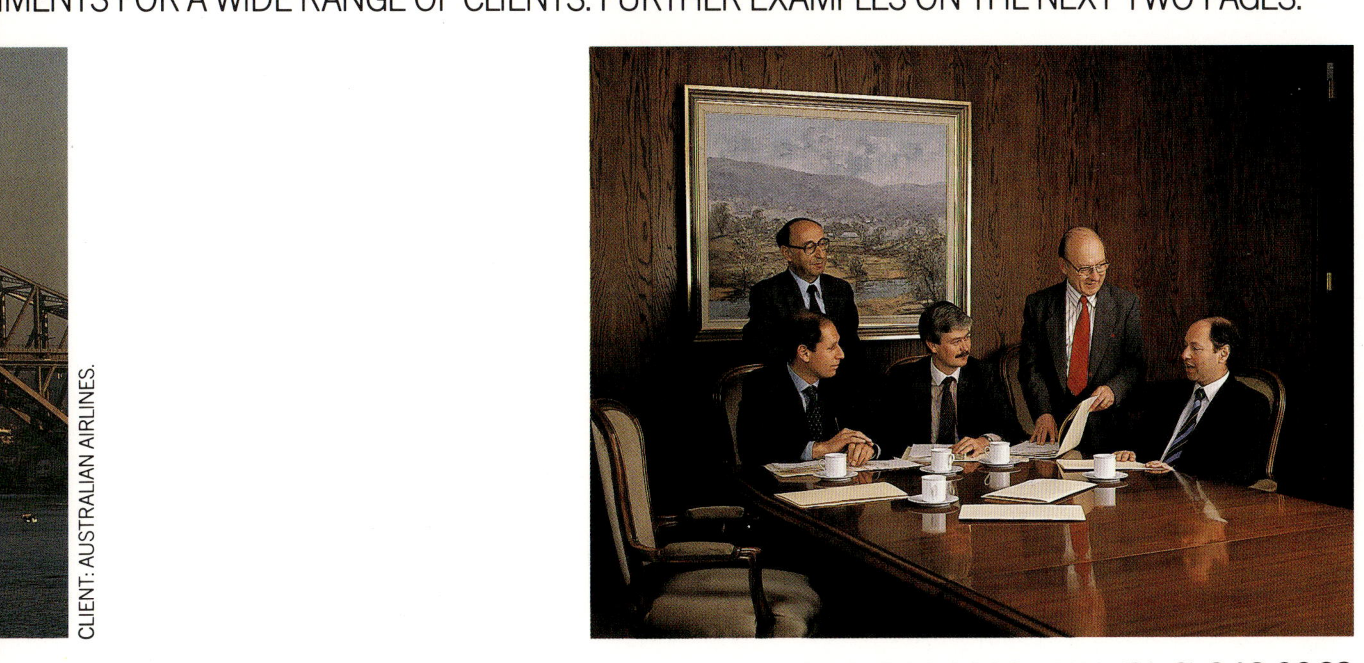

CLIENT: AUSTRALIAN AIRLINES.

CLIENT: HEINE MANAGEMENT LIMITED. DESIGNER: HANS BAUER.

CING. PETER WALTON PHOTOGRAPHY PTY LTD. TEL: (61-3) 848 9932 FAX: (61-3) 848 9968

PETER WALTON UNDERTAKES SPECIALLY COMMISSIONED PROJECTS SUCH AS

WITH STRONG EMPHASIS ON SCENICS. EXCELLENT FIRST HAND KNOWLEDGE OF MOST OF A

FOLIO AVAILABLE BY OVERNIGHT COURIER. A FLEXIBLE APPROAC

1991 CALENDAR FOR MALAYSIA AIRLINES. WIDE RANGE OF STOCK MATERIAL AVAILABLE FOR HIRE

ALIA'S SPECTACULAR PLACES, ESPECIALLY VALUABLE WHEN PLANNING LOCATION ASSIGNMENTS.

PRICING. PETER WALTON PHOTOGRAPHY PTY LTD. TEL: (61-3) 848 9932 FAX: (61-3) 848 9968

David McCarthy Photography Studio is situated at 3 Mowbray Terrace, East Brisbane, just 5 minutes from the CBD so parking is easy – although 80% of our work is "on location". Be it in coal mines, corporate board rooms, the Gold Coast, the chairman's office, building sites, factories, airports or from helicopters and airplanes anywhere.

We even go to Sydney!

But we much prefer it when we go to Cairns and the Barrier Reef islands and all points in between.

Client list includes: ANL, ACI, Baulderstone Hornibrook, Department of Justice, Metway Bank, Mobil Oil Co., Palmers Tube Mills, ERA Ray White, Colliers International, John Holland Group, BHP Steel, Jennings, SEQEB, Suncorp, Capital Airlines, GWA, Kinhill Cameron McNamara, Kwikasair, Steelmark …

1991 makes our 33rd year in professional photography – help make it a good one for us and we'll make good pictures for you.

David McCarthy Photography
Commercial and Advertising Photography
3 Mowbray Terrace,
East Brisbane. Qld. 4169.
Phone (07) 891 1222
Fax (07) 891 5848

David McCarthy Photography

Commercial and Advertising Photography 3 Mowbray Terrace, East Brisbane. Qld. 4169.
Phone (07) 891 1222 Fax (07) 891 5848

TOMEK & ERYK.

National Australia Bank Report 1988.

When the National Bank board meeting broke up in 1988, Tomek & Eryk needed just 7 minutes of the Board's time to capture the shot you see here.

It's become a classic in corporate Promotion because it's spontaneous, authoritative and attractive.

However, don't be misled into thinking 7 minutes was all the time needed to achieve a shot of this calibre.

The shot was researched, pre-lit, rehearsed right down to floor marks for each member, and the only thing left to chance was the individual facial expressions.

From the member's point of view, not one minute of their valuable time was wasted, and the result is a triumph.

This is indicative of the care Tomek & Eryk give to each assignment. Originally working as photojournalists in Poland, the team of Tomek & Eryk has become synonomous with a result that is creative and attractive. Now they work around the world with confidence – either as a team, or as self-sufficient individuals each injecting the result of their life's experiences into the frame, at the same time giving each shot an individual approach.

Wherever you need a location shot, if Tomek and Eryk are in the area, say, Asia, Europe, Australia or America, it's quite likely one of the team will be able to finish the job they're on and move onto your job and thus amortise travel expenses.

By discussing your project with Tomek & Eryk in the early concept stages, you will achieve an extra element of creativity.

The work on these pages gives you a taste of the range and prestige of Tomek & Eryk's work.

The agents listed will be happy to show you much more of their work.

National Australia Bank Report 1988. Designer: Robert Rosetzky.

15 Simmons Street, South Yarra, Victoria 3141 Australia 03) 827 5397 Fax: 03) 824 0483

New York agent 'Marzena' 212) 772 2522. Fax: 212) 249 6917 Brussells agent. Art Connection. Pierre Pativ 25) 37 4221.

Telecom Australia.

Inter-Continental Hotels. USA.

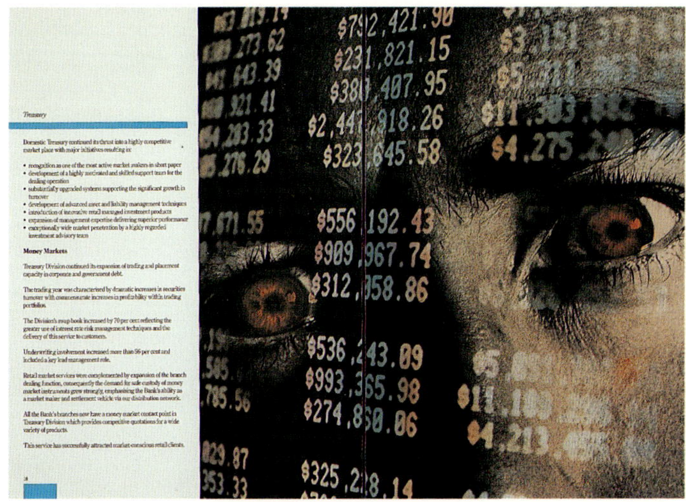

Annual Report to Staff 1987. State Bank Victoria.

Elders Annual Report 1989.

State Bank Billboard.

CORPORATE CONSULTANTS.

Ethel the Aardvark and other corporate communications

If you want corporate communications which are clear, persuasive, properly thought out and free of jargon, Alex and Paddy Stitt will be happy to help you. Does this mean funny pictures? Not necessarily. Some of our most serious work looks pretty lighthearted, but there's a lot more to our work than 'Life. Be in it' (though that's probably our best known).

We do absolutely straight annual reports for corporate giants. We make educational videos, design corporate images and write corporate brochures. We devise marketing plans and write proposals that help our clients to win business. We have prepared strategy documents for Government Ministries as well as consumer campaigns to support the strategies. We once wrote a 300 page submission for the ABT – and won a commercial FM licence with it.

Mostly, we write, design and produce our work ourselves, but sometimes Alex designs books, films, commercials, brochures and posters using other writers' words, and sometimes Paddy takes on writing assignments with other designers or other directors. Alex frequently writes and Paddy sometimes directs videos as well as writing them.

Often we do whole jobs without a hint of humour. But sometimes serious subjects can benefit from leavening, so we come up with ideas like Ethel, who was created to add good humour to otherwise difficult material in a book called "Ethel the Aardvark Goes Quantity Surveying".

You'll find us at 2 Hazeldon Place, South Yarra, 3141. Telephone (03) 826 8451. Fax (03) 827 3115.

Alexander Stitt & Partner

Ethel.
She starred in an otherwise serious publication about quantity surveying.

A complete graphic design service, from concept development through to print supervision. A thorough understanding of clients' needs with a comprehensive team of experts specialising in
corporate communications
visual identity programs
promotional material
editorial design
packaging
signage

THE · CORPORATE · STORY

The Corporate Story provides marketing, public relations and communications services to business. Established in 1985 to meet the needs of the professions, this small, specialist consultancy includes among its clients lawyers, accountants and financial advisers, architects, construction cost consultants, interior designers and engineers.
The Corporate Story also works in the areas of health, publishing and travel.
The firm is particularly noted for its expertise in written communication, winning recognition for its work on brochures, house magazines and a range of corporate communications.
The Corporate Story provides:

- Planned public relations programs.
- Communications strategies.
- Media liaison.
- PR and communication audits.
- Editorial, advertising copy and institutional writing.
- A full range of publication-related services.
- Speech writing.

Contact
Elaine McTaggart
Director
The Corporate Story
Suite 3
206 Cotham Road
Kew
Victoria 3101
Telephone: 03 817 5699
Facsimile: 03 816 9206

THE LANGUAGE OF PERSONAL IMAGE IN A CORPORATE ENVIRONMENT.

There was once an advertisement which read:

"Imagine you are all sitting around the boardroom table. Stark naked.

"How do you tell who the boss is?"

The answer: The man with the Parker pen, of course!

Jon Colleen Laing of Visual Contact has worked for years noting and refining the subtleties of personal communication through individual style. She has concluded that the majority of us discount and deny the power of our own presence.

Presence is surely made up of confidence, knowledge, security in one's self, value of self and an ease about one's appearance.

Do you feel comfortable with yourself, your personnel and your company or organisation on all occasions?

The smallest detail out of place can communicate your secret flaws. Opposite, we graphically illustrate an obvious flaw of fit and how it communicates to the observer.

Jon Colleen Laing recognises that gradual development is necessary for a client to feel confident in the advice given. She takes image beyond the obvious. By starting at the level they are currently presenting, she leads an organisation or individual step by step through theory, practical application and motivation. These steps depend on the extent of the brief, but they may include motivational awareness, lectures, seminars to large or small groups, uniform workwear or corporate wardrobe design.

Individual recommendations can be made on the development of an employment policy related to image.

In order to feel comfortable with the advice given, image development takes time, sensitivity, tolerance, awareness and commitment.

Jon's belief in personal service has established Visual Contact as one of Australia's leading consultants in creating confidence through image.

"It has long been an axiom of mine that the little things are infinitely the most important."

SHERLOCK HOLMES.

TO FIT OR NOT TO FIT.

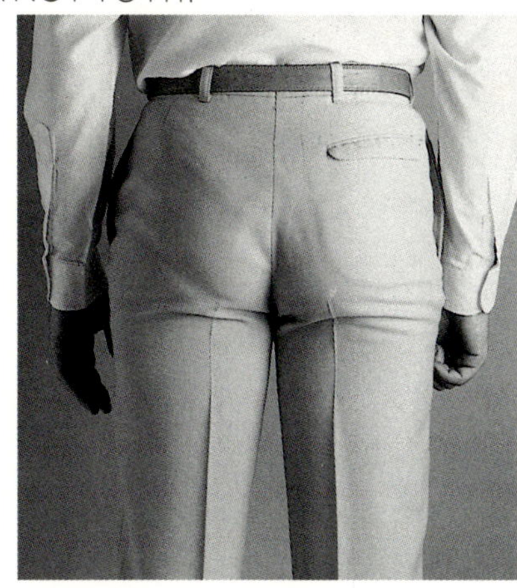

You don't have to be a Holmes or a Watson to notice a badly cut suit, a poor choice of tie, an inferior fabric, or a look which is just somehow "wrong".

Whilst fine-tuning a client's personal image is a Visual Contact speciality, it's the development of the total image which is regarded as a top priority.

Image in relation to professional position, using dress as a business strategy, and developing personal style within corporate limitations.

Jon Colleen Laing believes image begins at the top line of a company and makes its way to the reception staff and finally the all-important front entrance.

Visual Contact

THE SPECIALISTS IN PERSONAL IMAGE DEVELOPMENT

The Studio, 53 Charles Street, Fitzroy, Victoria 3065. Telephone (03) 419 9723.

DESIGN.

CRACKERJACK
DESIGN GROUP
PTY LIMITED
GROUND LEVEL
2 1 3 - 2 1 7
PALMER STREET
DARLINGHURST
N S W 2 0 1 0
TELEPHONE
3 3 2 2 8 6 6
FACSIMILE
3 3 1 3 6 3 5

The ethos
of art
and the ethos
of business
cannot be
reconciled

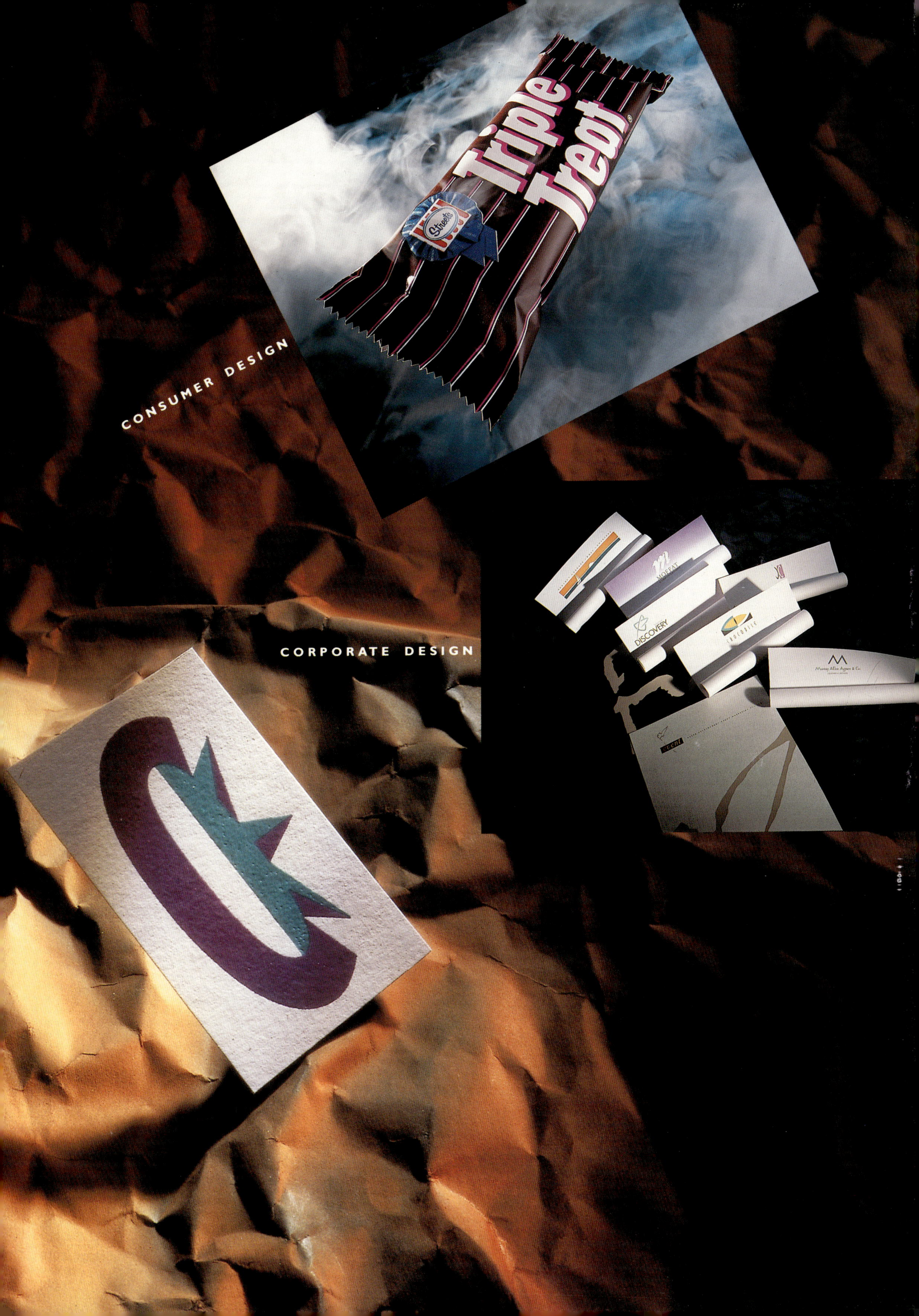

CONSUMER DESIGN

CORPORATE DESIGN

Graphic design and production in all areas of printing, to the highest standards.

Specialising in corporate literature and packaging.

Our approach is quiet, elegant, professional. And different. (You need to be different to be noticed. You need to be noticed to communicate effectively.)

We deal directly with clients and production people to ensure maximum control throughout each job.

We win awards for our work.

PICTURES BY MARK LLEWELLYNN

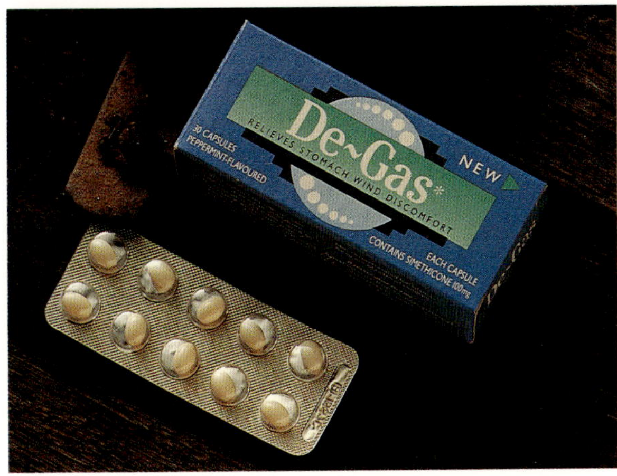

EVERYTHING *YOU EVER WANTED IN A* DESIGN GROUP BUT DIDN'T KNOW WHO TO ASK

Naturally, the first thing you need in a design group is creativity. But creativity on its own is not enough. You need a group big enough to offer the infrastructure and support to make the creativity effective. Creativity must go hand in hand equally with professional planning, account service, strategic solutions and image control. You may need a marketing led design group to help solve image problems whether for a brand, service or your entire company. ***Bluetree offers all of these things.***

WHAT WE CAN DO FOR YOU

At Bluetree we help plan your visual communications long term, help you structure your budgets for cashflow and affordability, and create a consistent image for your company, products and services.

Therefore your company's image will grow into a tangible asset.

Our expertise covers all areas of communications design, including corporate identity and logotype design and its management, innovative packaging design, stationery, annual reports, direct mail programmes, signage and interior design.

Once briefed we will control copywriting, typesetting, finished artwork and all aspects of film separations and print supervision. We will also select and contract photographers, illustrators, signmakers and a broad range of suppliers on your behalf.

WHY CHOOSE ONE DESIGN GROUP ABOVE ALL OTHERS?

There are many benefits in having just one design group handling all your visual communications:

•One company can provide a coherent service avoiding the inevitable breaks in continuity that occur using several design groups, or in the event of key members of your staff leaving.

•You have more control over your marketing activities.

•It gives you stronger buying power for printed material and lower overall costs.

•The single design group will develop an overall picture of the personality and direction of your company.

•You will need to brief only one company.

•It's easier to administrate from your point of view.

SMILE PLEASE

We've developed something called a Visual Audit, which is like a snapshot of the way your company presents itself to the outside world, from business cards and brochures through to signage and livery.

It is a report which is used as a springboard from which to make image planning and control decisions with specific recommendations on which part of your visual communications are liabilities, and which are assets.

LET'S TALK

If you'd like to know more, call Eugene Rea or Peter Wincott on 02 357 7966.

BLUETREE DESIGN CONSULTANTS

119 Cathedral Street, Woolloomooloo, NSW 2011.
Phone 02 357 7966 Fax 02 357 7965.

CREDENTIALS

Since its foundation in 1987 by partners Eugene Rea and Timothy Boydle, Bluetree has emerged as a new force in Australian design.

Clients include British Airways, Compaq Computer Australia, Johnson and Johnson, Lend Lease Corporation, Murdoch Magazines and Nestle.

Corlette Design is one of Australia's leading Graphic Design Consultancies and is proudly associated with some of the largest and most exciting companies in Australia and overseas.

Design is undoubtedly an essential element of a company's marketing mix. A good, innovative design incorporated across the spectrum will provide the edge or identity that can make a product or service a success in an ever more competitive market.

Since its inception in 1979, Corlette Design has been highly successful in creating effective visual solutions for its clients' increasingly demanding corporate and marketing objectives.

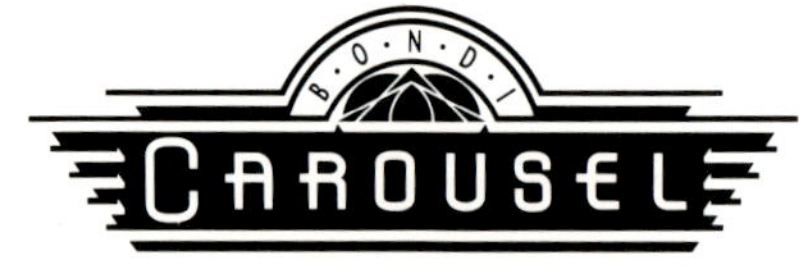

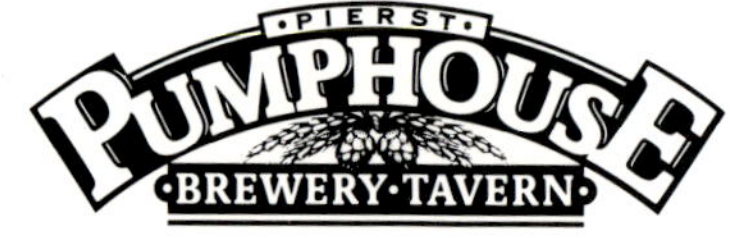

360 Pacific Highway

Crows Nest NSW 2065

Tel 02 439 4922

BONDI CAROUSEL

CORLETTE DESIGN

BATH GEL
SHAMPOO
BODY LOTION
CONDITIONER
SHOWER CAP
GOODNIGHT
The Regent

Max Robinson Design

Graphic design today plays an increasingly more powerful role in industry than ever before. From banks to boutiques, effective visual presentation strengthens the hand of advertisers and marketers in tough economic conditions.
Using intuition and imagination, the creative designer expresses the potential and positive aspects of a client's product.
Working with a client, as an integral part of the corporate family, a designer nurtures a company's image as it develops, from infancy to adulthood.
As part of a team, employing logical and efficient procedures, a design group offers business an invaluable tool for communication. Max Robinson Design is such a design group.

Suite 19
545 St Kilda Road Melbourne
Victoria 3004 Australia
Tel (03) 510 3000 Fax (03) 510 5185

1 *The Melbourne Lighter. Floating Restaurant*
2 *BM Marketing. Vending machine operators*
3 *Australian National Boxing Federation*
4 *Ace of Clubs. Licensed clubs own liquor range*
5 *Ritz Collection. Discount label of Hickory Fashions*
6 *ABM Plastics. Plastic sheeting manufacturer*
7 *Drops on the Rocks. Ready mixed Baitz cocktail*
8 *JFK Foods International. European fast foods*
9 *Dimensions. Personal improvement programs*
10 *HOA Investment Fund. Hospital property manager*
11 *House of Hops. Imported beer wholesaler*
12 *Yulara Tourist Resort. Ayers Rock leisure complex*
13 *Chemical Pump Industries. Pumping equipment*
14 *McCoppins Wine Pub. Bar and restaurant*
15 *Victorian Wine Press Club. Wine and food writers*

1

2

3

4

5

6

7

8

9

10

11

12

13

14

15

Redbank Winery

One of Australia's most reputable small wineries. Our brief was to provide an undeniably Australian, but sophisticated visual identity for these products, aimed primarily at the export market. The symbol evolved logically from our package designs.

Simon De Winter Socks

A young, dynamic manufacturer took the market leaders head on. He soon found his distinctive style was being imitated. We were asked to solve the problem. We recommended that his name alone become the image, and carried throughout the range.

Hospitals of Australia

A group of private hospitals in New South Wales and Victoria. Formed as a unit trust in 1986, it is now restructured into two trusts. The symbol represents units grouped protectively around a cross, and suggesting the shape of Australia.

Global Funds Management

Formed in 1987 after a management split with Oceanic, Global have been aggressive and innovative in the tough financial conditions of today. We have designed all their material since inception, including a wide range of prospectuses and new products.

Poster

Packaging

Press Kit

Brochures

Packaging

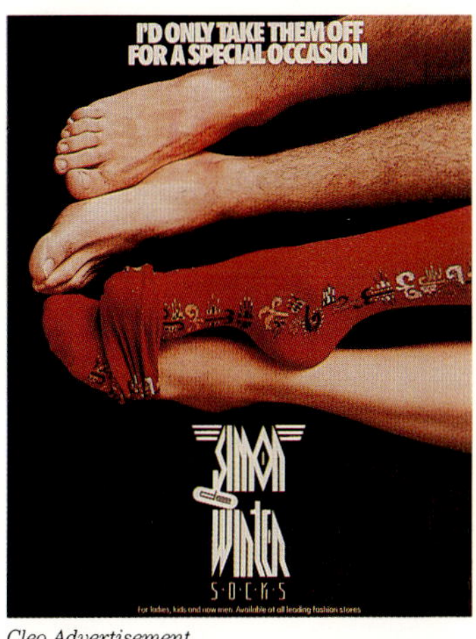

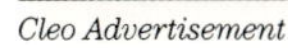
Cleo Advertisement

Carry Bag

1988 Annual Report

1989 Annual Report

1990 Annual Report

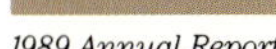

1988 Annual Report

1989 Annual Report (Recycled Paper)

1990 Annual Report (Recycled Paper)

BRIAN SADGROVE & ASSOCIATES, GRAPHIC DESIGN, 6 LITTLE PAGE ST

ALBERT PARK, VICTORIA 3206, TEL (03) 690 8977, FAX (03) 696 1337

B&B DESIGN PTY LTD
22 WELLINGTON STREET,
ST. KILDA,
VICTORIA 3182.
PHONE: (03) 529 8999
FAX: (03) 525 2207

CORPORATE DESIGN

NUTTSHELL GRAPHICS

Graphic Design Consultants

Nuttshell Graphics is a small, dedicated, team of professional graphic designers who offer a comprehensive service from conceptual development through to print supervision.

Headed by Sue Allnutt, the company draws on her many years experience in Australia and overseas teaching and practising graphic design. Since its foundation in 1985, Nuttshell Graphics has built up a significant reputation in the graphic design of corporate and visual identities, corporate publications, brochures, annual reports, ranges of stationery and logos.

The studio utilises the latest technological advances in graphic design with its own 'in-house' computer layout and typesetting facilities.

Clients vary from leading national and international companies to small businesses, conference organisations and museums. The approach to each client is a personal one. Individual needs are assessed and a close working relationship emerges. The product is tailored to meet intellectual, artistic and communication needs with an overall emphasis on quality.

Current clients include Amcor Limited, Amrad Corporation, Anti Cancer Council of Victoria, Coles Myer Limited, Datacraft Limited, E.P.A., Healesville Sanctuary, Mayne Nickless Limited, Premier Investments, T.A.B. and TransContinental Airlines of Australia.

Nuttshell Graphics Pty Ltd
51 Erskine Street North Melbourne 3051
Telephone 329 8988 Facsimile 326 5514

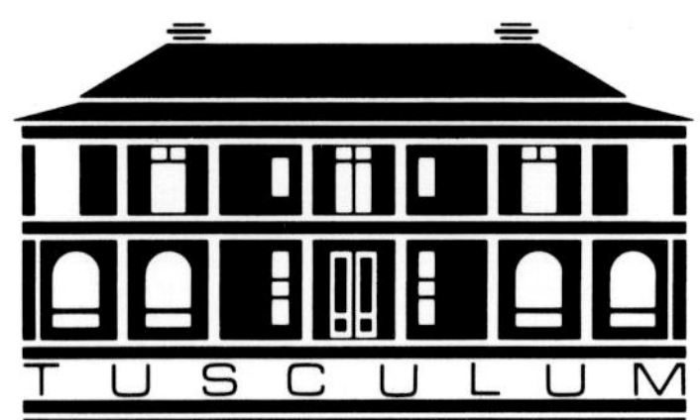

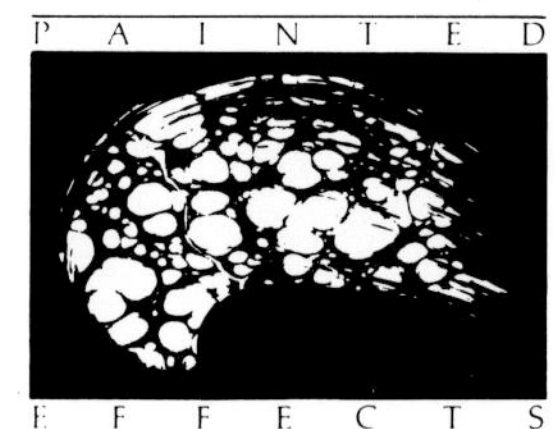

Richardson Design has a commitment to design which contributes to the marketing and business strategies of its clients. This commitment to effective design covers a spectrum from Annual Reports, Facilities and Capabilities Documents, Sales Promotion, Visual Identity Programmes, Packaging and Promotional Design.

The intent of our design approach is to prepare communications that are visually informative, stimulating and unique to the particular client. In support of our high creative standards, we offer thorough and effective project administration, resulting in a total service through all stages of consultation, design and production.

RICHARDSON DESIGN P/L

67 HARRIS STREET

PYRMONT

SYDNEY

NSW 2009

TEL: (02) 552 4165

FAX: (02) 552 4154

Send for the book.

Billy Blue Group.

Pragmatic Creativity.

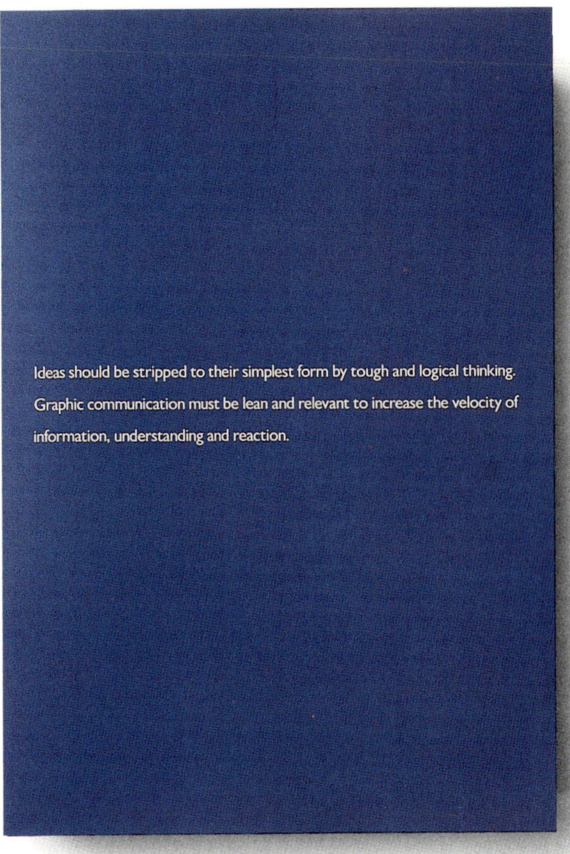

Billy Blue Group
PO Box 728
North Sydney 2059
Facsimile 957 2842

Name

Company

Address

Postcode

L I V I N G S T O N E

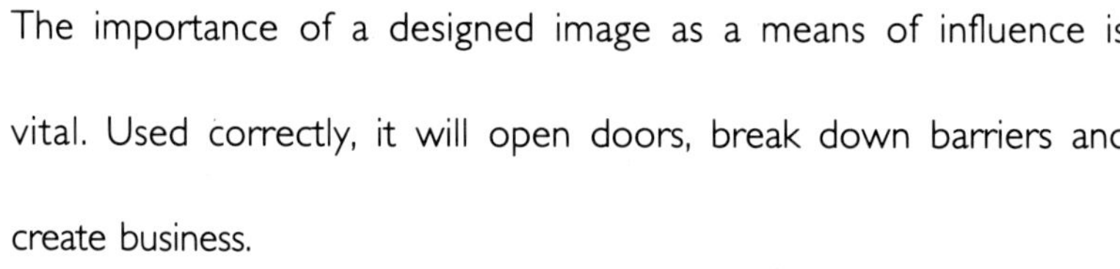

The importance of a designed image as a means of influence is vital. Used correctly, it will open doors, break down barriers and create business.

Livingstone Clark develops images which create a desired response using visual media. Essentially, we are an image consultancy specialising in corporate graffiti.

We look outside accepted boundaries to find solutions rather than rely on the obvious which can be dull, invisible and therefore, ineffective.

The result is a powerful, deliberate and effective form of communication which is activated by one of the strongest human senses: sight.

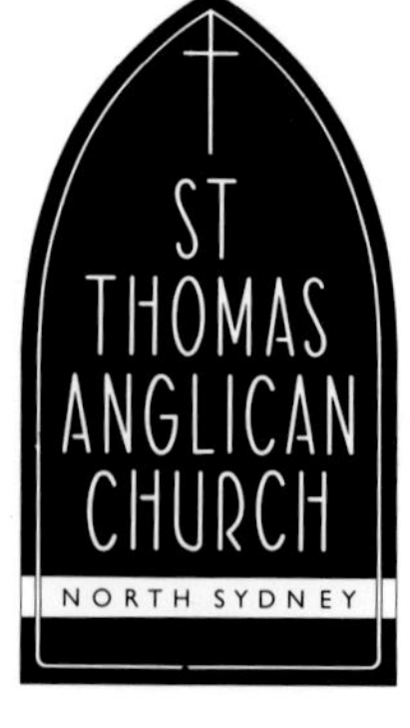

Livingstone Clark The Factory Suite 1 165 Walker Street North Sydney NSW 2060 Phone (02) 957 2601 Fax (02) 929 8676

C L A R K

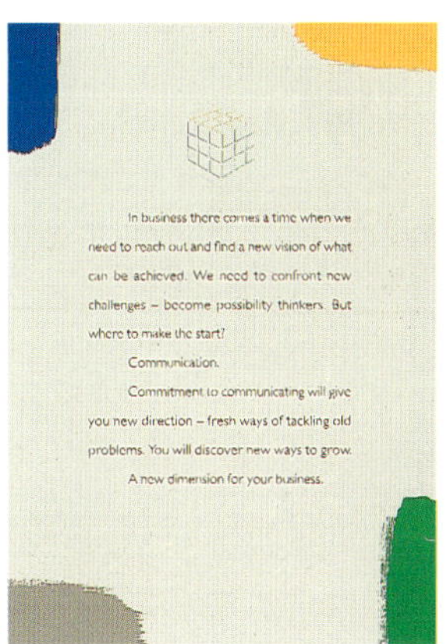

Please call for our complimentary brochure

InterGraphiq's standing in the design world is based on the philosophy that today's designers need a disciplined and business like approach to design. Commitment to this philosophy has seen Carola Easte establish her client base with some of Australia's prominent companies.

InterGraphiq specialises in corporate design development. Commissions range from the total corporate image programme to any aspect of a company's design or image requirement, including corporate stationery, identity and product manuals, signage systems, annual reports, corporate profiles, product brochures and packaging.

A broad spectrum of industry experience includes chemical, plastics, insurance, legal and finance, tourism, retailing, government and semi government, property development, agriculture and animal health, pharmaceutical, cosmetics and general manufacturing.

The studio deals not only with direct clients, but also through advertising agencies, public relations and marketing consultancies.

InterGraphiq has the ability to quickly interpret and reflect a client's needs, embracing both the marketing objectives and the corporate goals through a designer's skills.

Carola Easte believes quality, originality and a strong commitment to client service are the basis for the success and continued performance of her design studio.

CORPORATE DESIGN DEVELOPMENT

44 DOCKER STREET RICHMOND 3121

TEL 03 428 8225 FAX 03 427 7295

MARINA MIRAGE
GOLD COAST
MARINA MIRAGE
PORT DOUGLAS

WITH COMPLIMENTS

POISON
Panoctine
5 Litres
POISON
Saprol
Fungicide
5 Litres

Adstract Art is a Melbourne-based graphic design consultancy established in 1984 and headed by Paul Andrews.
It provides a complete design service, backed by the latest computer graphics and publishing capability.
The company's marketing-oriented approach, creativity and close understanding of its clients' communication requirements produces cost-effective, highly professional design solutions.
Adstract Art has established a reputation for a very high standard of service and design, with experienced designers personally supervising each job through every stage, from first rough to printing.
Their ability to adapt design disciplines to any project application ensures successful services in corporate and visual identities, logos, corporate publications, annual reports, newsletters, brochures, catalogues, packaging and signage.
Adstract Art's diverse range of clients includes small and large businesses in the manufacturing, retail, industrial, advertising and commercial spheres.

ADSTRACT ART

Adstract Art Pty. Ltd.

93-95 George Street

Fitzroy Victoria 3065

Telephone 03/417 2163

Facsimile 03/416 1660

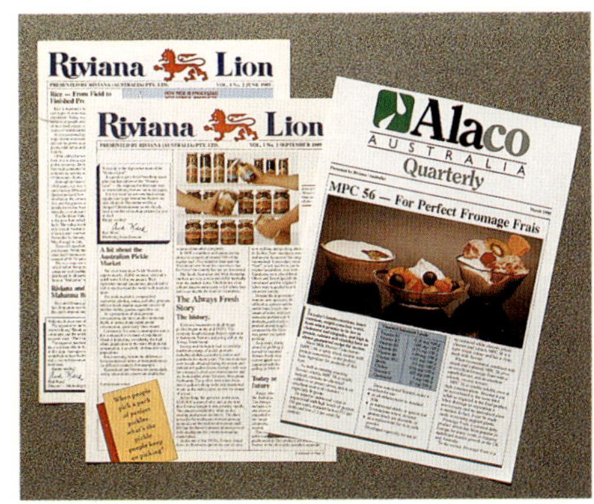

Advertising Artwork

& Graphic Design.

"Good design is good for business". Adhering to this basic premise has seen one Melbourne design studio grow from a one man operation nearly a decade ago to currently showcasing its work on the boardroom tables of some of Australia's major corporations.

With high profile clients from the Melbourne Olympic Committee, to Herbert Adams, Wedgwood, ICI, State Bank Victoria, the Board of Works, the Urban Land Authority,the Victorian Goverment Major Projects Unit, Ford Australia, Australia Post, National Mutual and Woodside Petroleum, Russell Bevers Design has certainly come a long way.

Russell Bevers sees corporate design and corporate imagery as basically a fusion of creative and marketing thinking.

For Russell Bevers the same design principles apply in the design of a company identity, a corporate brochure or annual report.

Established marketing principles combined with well researched methods of visual communication are used to create an image and establish visual standards that will be carried through from corporate mark to signage, print, uniforms, vehicles and media....right down to how the receptionist answers the phone.

It is evident in Russell Bevers' creative output for the Urban Land Authority. From logo to Annual Report, special projects literature and newsletter , a consistent corporate identity underlies all.

It is present too in the design consultancy's work for National Mutual where sound design enhances and complements an established corporate identity.

For Russell Bevers Design there must be a conscious design philosophy. According to Russell Bevers himself, "A good design will reflect the personality of the client. To achieve this the designer must have a thorough understanding of the client company's individual personality. From the company's own philosophy and goals will come the ideas that will achieve the visual identity."

And this identity must be relevant. "Creativity must have only one objective. The correctness of the idea for the project in hand. It is easy to grab the attention of someone, once that attention has been gained the message that comes through must be right. This is the heart of the matter and the most difficult goal to achieve. In other words, if the idea doesn't work, the designer has failed.

"It's a matter of a combination of logic and intuition", says Russell Bevers. "The application of logic identifies the problem for the designer, and helps establish the ground rules leading to a solution. However, it takes that extra creative spark, that personal style....call it what you will, that produces the idea that is unique, truly original, that stands out from the crowd!"

The formula seems to be working. Russell Bevers Design today boasts a healthy client list and a solid reputation for a high standard of workmanship.

An important factor in this success could also be that, as a design studio, Russell Bevers Design prides itself on retaining the personal touch that marked those simple beginnings.

"We've never been a design 'factory'", says Russell Bevers. "Everybody in this company can discuss and actually carry out design. Our clients find it reassuring to know they can communicate directly with the person who does the design work."

It's a commitment to service that makes for a very flexible and efficient operation. The staff of qualified graphic designers are all able to deal directly with clients and suppliers. A delegation of responsibility that ensures continuity for each project from inception to completion, making, in Russell Bevers' view, for more effective communication between client and designer.

In an everchanging, complex world, more visually aware than ever before, a combination of sound corporate design philosophy and "hands on' personal approach has seen this studio come a long way from its simple beginnings. Though they'd probably tell you it's been by design.

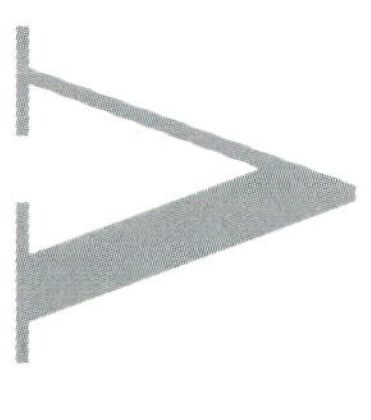

RUSSELL BEVERS DESIGN PTY LTD 20 Liddiard Street Hawthorn 3122

Olympic Schools Project - Vic Health / Melbourne Olympic Committee

Annual Report - Board of Works

Progress report on Docklands Redevelopment - Major Projects Unit

C Data 86 - Australian Bureau of Statistics

Williamstown Rifle Range Redevelopment - Urban Land Authority

Urban Land Authority

Good design gets results

For good results get our brochure.

RITCHIE THORBURN DESIGN (02) 692 0566 CORPORATE REPORTS AND PROFILES PRODUCT BROCHURES IDENTITIES

LEND LEASE CORPORATION LIMITED

1988 ANNUAL REPORT

RIEGEL PAPER PTY LTD
RIEGEL PAPER PTY LTD
Riegel Paper (S.A.) Pty. Ltd.
15 Rose Street, Mile End, South Australia 5031
Tel. (08) 352 3122 Facsimile (08) 352 8925
With Compliments
RIEGEL Incorporated in Victoria PAPER PTY LTD
Gary Dorman
Victorian Manager
32 Healey Road, Dandenong, Victoria, Australia, 3175
Telephone (03) 794 0444, Facsimile (03) 794 5088
ORANGE FRUIT JUICE DRINK
Thickened Cream
VANILLA CUSTARD
The Ad Shop
A
PTY LTD

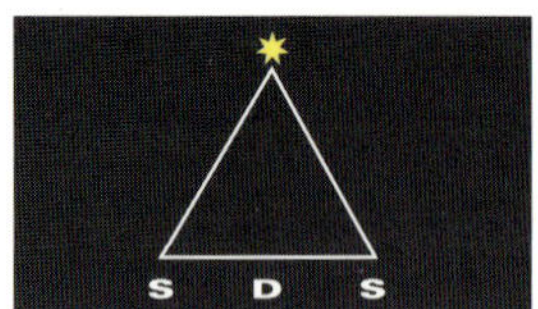

VACC

Motor Industry Update

New models fuel super Show

OnTheBall Design is geared to master any project challenge – from a single page promotional piece to a full-scale corporate identity program.

Being fully computerised doesn't mean that we just do desktop publishing. As Designers, we put Design first. As we design, we're also typesetting, illustrating and producing finished artwork. Our efficient technique means that less time is spent on manual labour, which starts to save you money. Our skills guarantee you the

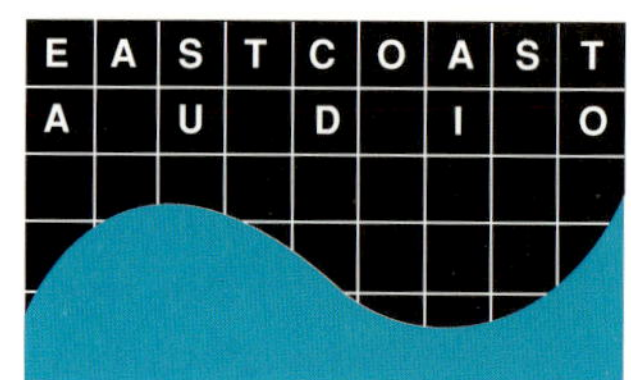

very best quality reproduction from bromides, film or plate material.

We have a hard-won reputation for producing sensible, effective design solutions that go to work immediately. With clients like Ansett, Hoechst, National Mutual and VACC we have to be OnTheBall with our design!

Whether you're a large or small company, call Andrew Willox on 03 326 6666 to find out more about how we can help you.

FLETT HENDERSON & ARNOLD

SPECIALISING IN THE AREAS OF ▲ CORPORATE IDENTITY DESIGN ▲ ENVIRONMENTAL SIGNAGE ▲ CORPORATE LITERATURE

DESIGN CONSULTANTS

F H A

Melbourne 'Alma' Unit One 663 Victoria Street Abbotsford Victoria 3067 Australia Telephone (03) 429 6888 Facsimile (03) 429 9171
Sydney Level Four 20 Alfred Street Milsons Point New South Wales 2061 Australia Telephone (02) 954 0300 Facsimile (02) 954 0438

Asprey Di Donato Design is a small company. No account executives, no marketing managers, no sales reps. These days more and more people are coming to

ASPREY DI DONATO DESIGN

realize the obvious advantages in dealing with smaller design studios. Not only is the service personalised, but also the pricing structure is a little more realistic.

Our philosophy as a design studio involves developing a close working relationship with our clients in order to maintain direct and personal communication during production, and ultimately to ensure that the finished job fulfils the client's needs as comprehensively as possible.

Being fully computerized enables us to attain an extremely high level of speed and accuracy without sacrificing our commitment to dynamic and innovative design as a successful marketing tool. This uncompromising attitude is an essential part of our work ethic, ensuring a consistently high standard of design across a wide variety of work including corporate identity, corporate profiles, annual reports, brochures, house magazines and packaging.

ASPREY DI DONATO DESIGN

107 NICHOLSON STREET EAST BRUNSWICK VICTORIA 3057
TELEPHONE (03) 388 0543 FACSIMILE (03) 388 1467

THE RIGHT COMPANY.

Matching the right design Company with your Company is important if you want to produce a quality, informative, up-to-date company or annual report. You need to know that the selected Design Company can produce everything you require and more.

You need to know they will produce within your budget and on time and also have the ability to be flexible as to ideas, and the way to show those ideas. Smooth co-operation is important and will eventuate in a better job all round.

When making the selection, the majority of corporate communicators use both interviews and samples. Word of mouth comes into the picture – but not to any large degree. Having found a design company, most corporations tend to use that design company for several years. Five years minimum is not unusual. Among the main reasons for returning to the same design company is one of empathy and holding a tight line to budgets.

Many corporate managers tend to favour the smaller design companies where they can achieve a relationship with the principals of that company, who may play an active role in the preparation of the annual report.

The process of producing an annual report is labour intensive between the Corporation managers and the design company. Most managers prefer to deal direct with the design company. They also expect to meet with the dcsigner at least once a week through the formative stages, and even through the processing time.

Whatever rapport is established in the early stages of the relationship sets the scene for most future dealings. The effect of a smooth, harmonious relationship will be reflected in the end result. However, sometimes stormy passages through the design stage result in exciting stimulating work which produces surprising and often extremely noteworthy results. Creativity can reflect a go-ahead, adventurous company.

The vast majority of corporations are likely to review the work of several design groups before making their final choice. Some companies review up to ten before choosing. This is an extremely wasteful exercise for all concerned, if the survey is labour intensive.

At certain times of the financial year some smaller design companies simply don't have the capacity to attract new business because of ongoing work and a series of prospective clients demanding "submissions". The dilemma here is that if the designer doesn't play ball, the company won't have a hope of gaining the prospective client. But when the chance is one in ten, they really have to take the gamble as to whether they get involved or to concentrate on getting the best out of the actual work in hand.

GOOD TIMING.

With the design of an annual report averaging up to two months and the actual production taking between three and six months, all the selection processes need to be in place well before release date.

There are too many companies whose executives know they have to produce a report for the financial year, but continually leave the preparation with the design company until the 'Figures are out'.

This is a far from ideal way to produce a piece of communication which ideally would do much more than publish the figures. It is this length of time which also encourages clients to stay where they are.

When a design company takes on the task of producing a report, quotes must take into account the time spent in client meetings – as well as all other costs. On average, companies meet the designer or design team between five and ten times. Some take up to fifteen meetings to finalise general concepts and directions, some even more. However, all this must be tempered by what is essential and what is 'getting to know you' as sometimes meetings are planned without any real point and can be wasteful in terms of time and energy.

It's obvious that design companies need to be as good at verbal communication as they are in their chosen field of design.

DEMAND AND SUPPLY.

When choosing suppliers for the annual report the choices are usually made by the design company with the corporation occasionally getting involved. If the client is interested in this process, it is important to have your choices clearly designated with samples of the supplier's work available. When moving to a new photographic or illustrative style from a previous piece of communication it can be politic to inform the client of the reasons and expected results.

Because many more people are au fait with photography, clients are sometimes keen to recommend their own chosen photographer. This can cause great conflicts with the designer who may believe that a particular photographer won't give him the desired effect, whereas the person they recommend has been chosen for a specific purpose.

However, with illustrators, design companies generally have a much freer hand as it is accepted that they have more intimate knowledge of the techniques which vary so enormously. Clients would do well to follow the advice of the design company if the final result is to enhance the initial concept in the best possible way.

Even when a corporation employs its own Public Relations company, it generally doesn't involve that company in the writing of its report, preferring to use an 'outside' writer. Many of these writers work freelance for a series of designers, but sometimes work independently with the Corporation which then hands on the copy to the designer. Ideally there would be a cohesive approach for the optimum result.

Choosing a typesetter in most cases is left to the design firm and today many designers have their own computerised typesetting facilities.

Choice of paper stocks can greatly influence the look of the finished job and as with all aspects, varies with the fashion of the moment, the budget and what is available.

When it comes to which printer is chosen, again it is quite common for the Corporation to have a 'pet' printer, who has worked with them from the year dot, or has some other prior arrangement with the client.

As with other choices, this can cause problems because ideally the designer would choose the printer and have an intimate knowledge of their skills and efficiency. If they have to use the 'Client's printer' there is often a lack of an ongoing relationship which can lead to misunderstandings.

Whilst it can be difficult for a client to step back from these areas, he or she should keep in mind they have chosen a designer for their specific skills and acknowledged areas of expertise. Choosing the best supplier is ideally left to the designer because they know the result they are aiming for, and generally are on common ground.

THE PICTURES.

It appears that colour photography is the most popular choice for depicting products and people.

Colour charts and graphs run into second place with most companies.

Black and white photography is also

popular and takes third spot, unfortunately seen as a poor relation, simply because in many instances the reason for its use is purely cost.

Illustration runs fourth as a choice for visuals in most reports, however, the whims of fashion play a large part in its use.

Right now, illustration is probably chosen more than at any other time in the history of such reports, particularly as the design takes on a more creative, imaginative approach.

At long last, many corporations are seeing their reports as more than just a group of figures which they must produce – by Company Law.

They recognise that as a means of communication it must reflect and record the actions of the company in the most favourable light. Thus colour photography or illustration is the most popular means of communication. Black and white photography is used in about 20% of reports with black and white illustration hardly used at all except in illustrative graphs etc.

Photography of CEOs is still popular with most companies and is seen as a very important part of the annual report. However, the traditional photo of the CEO posed passively in his or her office seems to be fading from the scene.

This is an area where portrait photographers and photo journalists with good communication skills and an eye for getting the most out of a subject will win through.

In some reports, these photos are the only photos and thus interesting backgrounds and techniques can lift the overall design to new heights.

THE PRINTING.

Colour wins of course.

Very few corporate reports will use only two colours. Four colour printing is popular with many, as is five colour printing, but most reports will feature six colours to achieve the 'right' look.

Most reports will usually run into 5,000 copies at least, with many going up to 25,000 copies. About one quarter run up to as many as 50,000 copies.

Top quality, attention to detail, and true craftsmanship are all crucial elements, as well as meeting the inevitable tight deadline.

THE FINISH.

Lamination is as popular as ever, especially for covers and 'special' introduction pages. Embossing is still very popular with over 30% of companies.

New techniques are constantly being explored by both the designers and the production boffins. Some of these results are most interesting, however some supply shock tactics which are not always beneficial to the overall communication.

Being selective in the choice of progressive finishes, sometimes brings the surprise of re-introducing a long-forgotten technique which fell from fashion, has come full circle, and again looks exciting, such as marbling and hand made papers.

ANNUAL REPORT REPORT.

Twice now, Tomasetti Paper has gathered together a collection of commercially printed pieces of corporate communication and exhibited them around Australia.

The following pages show a selection from The 2nd International Corporate Report Exhibition. However, as we're depicting the best of Australia's work in CBD, we've only selected those produced in Australia.

As Australia's corporate paper specialist, Tomasetti's role to act as a catalyst in exposing and stimulating clients to the best corporate reporting will continue.

As corporations come to expect effectiveness and sophistication from their graphic communication, each publication must reflect corporate philosophy and achievements. At the same time, contemporary design, printing craftsmanship and creative use of fine papers, will bring to life the ambitions, the products, the people, and the profiles of Australia's leading corporations.

STATE BANK OF VICTORIA
1988 ANNUAL REPORT

Designer: Graphic Outline, Yanis Audrins, Melbourne.
Printer: Mercedes Waratah Press, Melbourne.
Paper: Cover: Tomasetti White A Artboard 260 gsm.
Text: Tomasetti White A Dull 150 gsm.
Production: 4 colour. 2 special plus spot gloss varnish.
Press: Akiyama 8 colour.

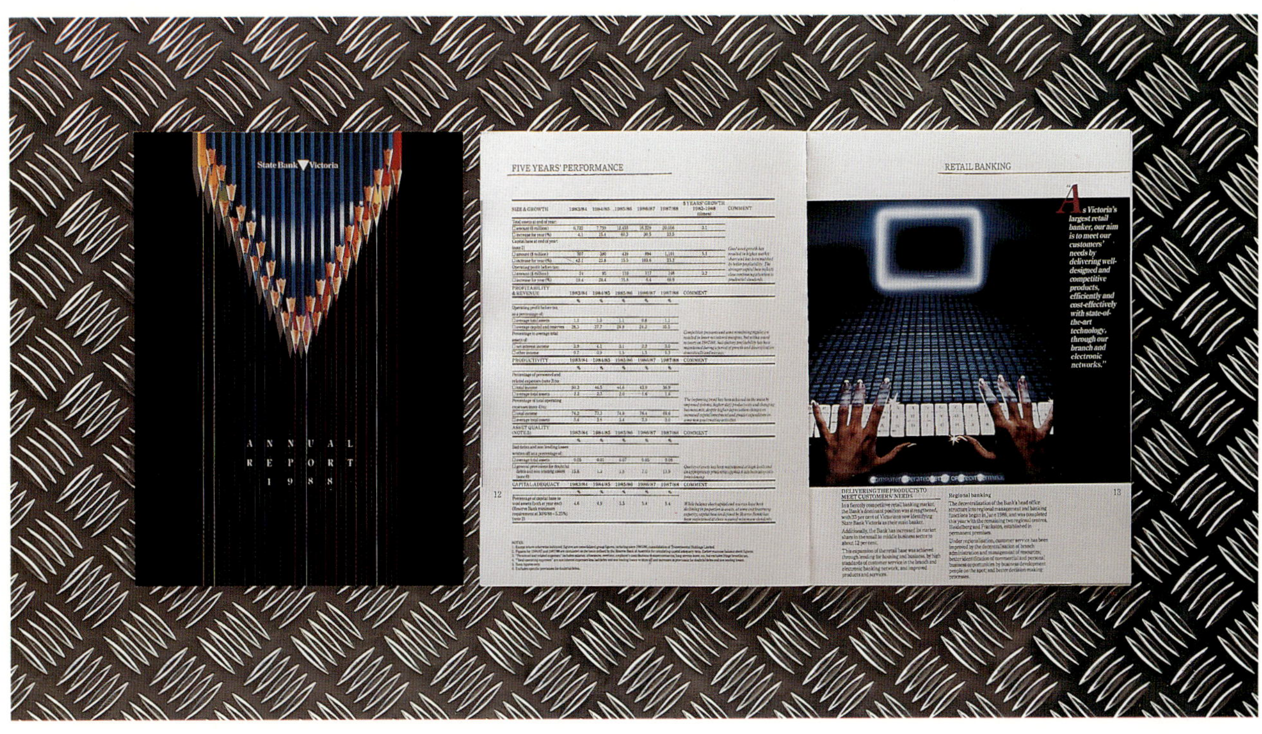

Designer: Graphic Outline, Melbourne.

GLOBAL FUNDS MANAGEMENT LTD 1989 ANNUAL REPORT

Designer: Max Robinson Design, Melbourne.
Printer: Victorian Printing.
Paper: Cover: Passport.
Text: Tomasetti White A Dull.
Financials: Passport. Recycled.
Reproduction: Prism Reproduction.
Production: 4 colour process and one special colour and gloss varnish.
Presses: Cover & Financials: Heidelberg 72 V
Text: Lithrone 440.

DESIGNER'S COMMENT

Max Robinson:

"The executive at Global Funds Management, a Sydney based financial company, are very environmentally conscious. They developed one of Australia's first Ethical funds (YWCA).

For their 1989 Annual Review, we proposed an environmental theme which they readily accepted.

We printed the financial section and the cover on recycled stock, when it was not at all certain colour would work, and the text on 170 gsm White A Dull from Tomasetti."

Max Robinson Design, Melbourne.

PIPER ALDERMAN PROFILE

Designer:	Ian Kidd Design, Adelaide.
Printer:	Visual Impressions, Adelaide.
Paper:	Cover: Tomasetti Ikonorex Dull 300 gsm. Text: Tomasetti Ikonorex Dull 150 gsm.
Production:	Cover: 4 colour process. Text: 4 colour process plus 1 PMS.

Ian Kidd Design, Adelaide.

JAMES CHRISTOU & PARTNERS

Designer: Turner Graphics, Perth.
Printer: Frank Daniels, Perth.
Paper: Cover: Tomasetti White Artboard 360 gsm.
Text: Tomasetti Ikonorex Dull 200 gsm.
Reproduction: Negs & scans: Quadrascan Graphics.
Production: Cover: 4 colour process plus gloss laminate.
Text: 4 colour process plus 1 PMS colour.
Presses: Cover: Komori L 26.
Text: Roland RFJ 33.

DESIGNER'S COMMENT

Paul R Dennis, Turner Design:

"James Christou & Partners is an architectural practice which has experienced considerable success in the design of waterside hospitality and resort based developments. In order to capitalise on those projects and promote its services, both in Australia and abroad, the company required a creative and prestigious representation of its design philosophy, range of services and recent work.

The design required a sensitive integration of project photography and architectural renderings. These pictorial elements were supported by a scheme of additional graphics to provide a visual unity for the brochure and allow for future expansion of content."

Turner Graphics, Perth.

LINKON GROUP PROFILE, "FROM THE GROUND UP"

Designer: City Graphic, Melbourne.
Printer: The Craftsman Press, Melbourne.
Paper: Cover: Tomasetti White A Artboard 260 gsm
Text: Tomasetti White A Dull 150 gsm.
Production: Cover: 4 colour process plus 1 PMS.
Text: 4 colour process plus 1 special.
Press: Heidelberg Speedmaster 5 colour 40".

Designer: City Graphic, Melbourne.

LEND LEASE 1989 ANNUAL REPORT

Designer: Horniak & Canny, Sydney.
Printer: The Pot Still Press, Sydney.
Paper: Cover: Tomasetti White A Artboard 310 gsm.
Text: Tomasetti White A Dull 170 gsm.
Production: 6 colour plus spot gloss varnish.
Press: Heidelberg Speedmaster 6 colour 40″.

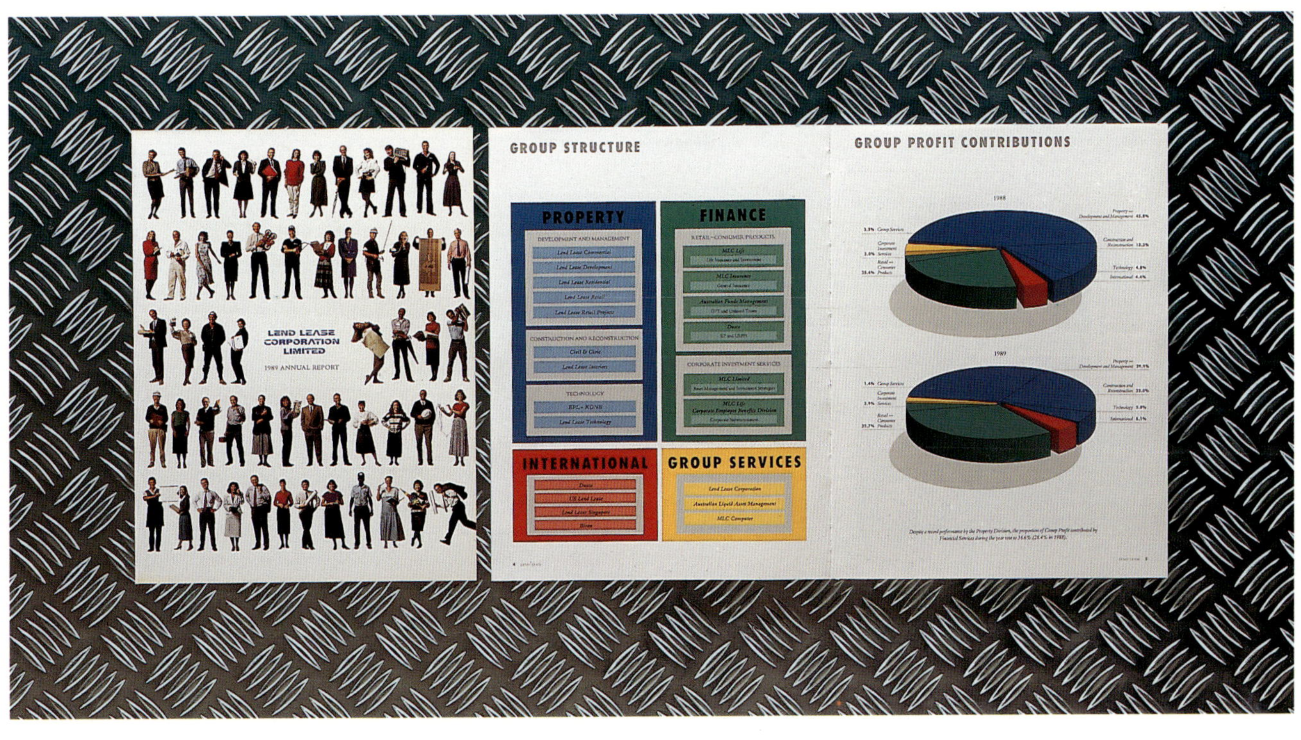

Designer: Horniak & Canny, Sydney.

NATIONAL COMMERCIAL UNION
1988 ANNUAL REPORT

Designer: Emery Vincent Associates, Melbourne.
Co-ordination: Rollo Corporate Communication.
Photography: Karl Schwerdtfeger.
Printer: Southbank Printing Services, Melbourne.
Paper: Cover: Tomasetti White A Artboard 260 gsm.
Text: Tomasetti Ikonorex Dull 170 gsm.
Production: 4 colour process throughout
Press: Heidelberg Speedmaster 4 colour 40".

DESIGNER'S COMMENT
Garry Emery, Emery Vincent Associates:

"Our objective here was to utilise black and white reportage photography sourced from newspaper files to represent specific products and services such as fire insurance, motor accident insurance and marine insurance, that are offered by National Commercial Union.

The black and white press photographs have been placed into a new context, orchestrated by the designers, and photographed to enrich in colour the presentation and reinforce the message to shareholders and the financial community.

The information is conveyed through classic typographical means."

Emery Vincent Associates, Melbourne.

JOONDALUP 1987 ANNUAL REPORT

Designer:	Chameleon Designs, Perth.
Printer:	Imperial Printing Company, Perth.
Paper:	Cover: Tomasetti Ikonorex Dull White 300 gsm. Text: Tomasetti Ikonorex Dull Ivory 170 gsm. Financial: Tomasetti Ikonorex Dull White 170 gsm.
Reproduction:	Scans & Plates: Quadrascan.
Production:	Cover Front: 4 colour process plus PMS Green, PMS Red, Gold Foil and Gloss Supersheen. Cover Inside: PMS Green and Ivory. Text: 4 colour process. Financial: 2 colour, PMS Green and Black. Press: Heidelberg MOVP. Inks: Dai Nippon.

Chameleon Designs, Perth.

DATACRAFT 1990 ANNUAL REPORT

Designer: Nuttshell Graphics Melbourne.
Printer: Vega Press Melbourne.
Paper: Cover: Tomasetti White A Artboard 260 gsm.
Text: Tomasetti White A Dull 150 gsm.
Financials: 128 gsm.
Production: 4 colour process.
Press: Komori Lithrone 40.
Inks: Toyo.

DESIGNER'S COMMENT
Sue Allnutt. Nuttshell Graphics:

"The brief asked for a positive, strong image to reflect the successful year Datacraft has had.

I felt to carry out the illustrations using computer generated images was both exciting and appropriate, given the nature of Datacraft's business, a large proportion of which, is involved with computer networking."

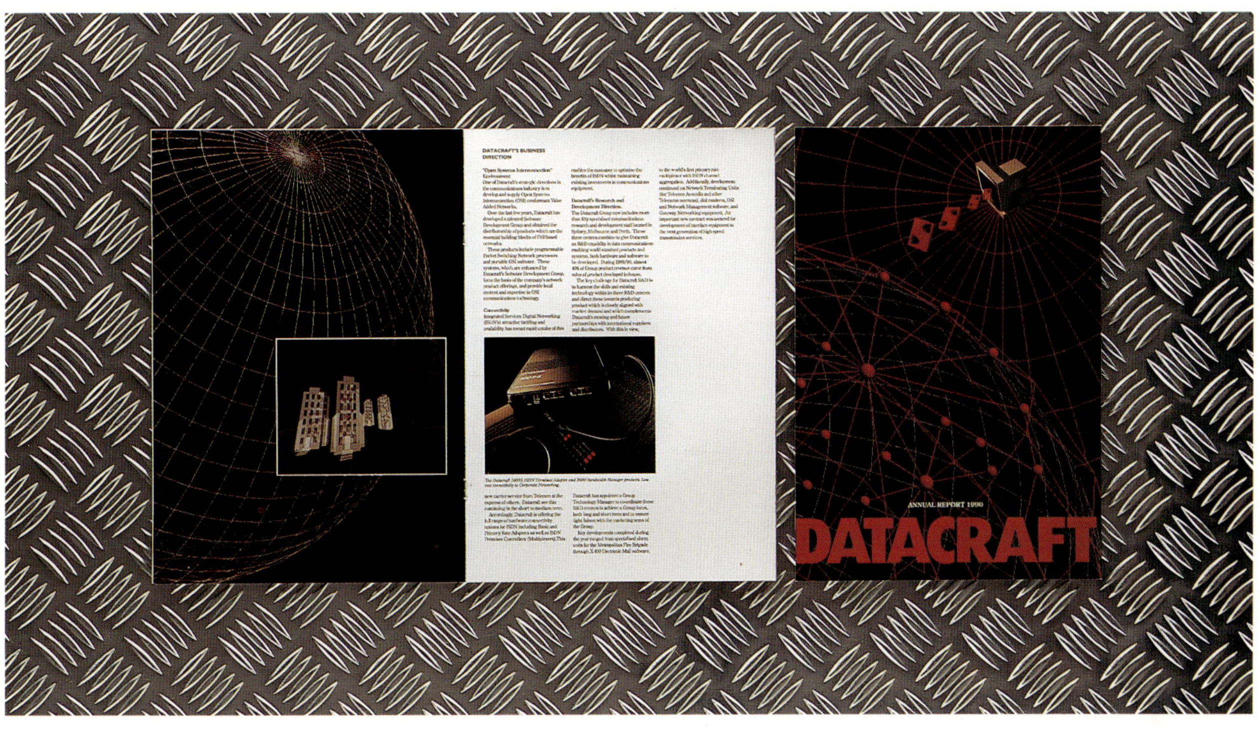

Nuttshell Graphics, Melbourne.

ANZ 1988 ANNUAL REPORT

Designer: Avenue Design, Melbourne.
Produced By: D. L. Hauser & Assoc, Melbourne.
Printer: Canberra Press, Melbourne.
Paper: Cover: Tomasetti White A Artboard 260 gsm.
Text: Ikonofix Matt WEB 135 gsm.
Production: Cover: 4 colour process Celloglazed
and Silver foil stamped by Avon Graphics.
Text: 4 colour process.
Press: Heidelberg 5 colour WEB.

Avenue Design, Melbourne.

HOSPITALS OF AUSTRALIA
1989 ANNUAL REPORT

Designer: Max Robinson Design, Melbourne.
Printer: Victorian Printing.
Paper: Cover: Tomasetti White A Artboard.
Text: White A Dull.
Reproducation: Prism Reproduction.
Production: 4 colour process + one special colour + gloss varnish.
Presses: Cover: Heidelberg 72V.
Text: Lithrone 440.

DESIGNER'S COMMENT
Max Robinson:

"Hospitals of Australia is a Trust Fund owning 13 private hospitals, mainly in NSW.

Following a reconstruction in 1989, HOA Investment Fund was created to own the assets, whilst the day-to-day operation of the hospitals remained with the original company.

We have designed the corporate identity for this group and their reports since inception in 1986.

For the 1989 report, we featured a photo story by Rowan Fotheringham of Strathfield Hospital, the first purpose-built private hospital in the Sydney area for more than a decade."

Max Robinson Design, Melbourne.

NORTHERN STAR HOLDING
(CHANNEL 10) 1988 ANNUAL REPORT

Designer: Elda Charous (Kameruka), Sydney.
Printer: Southbank Printing Services, Melbourne.
Paper: Cover: Tomasetti White A Artboard 310 gsm.
Text: Tomasetti Ikonorex Dull 170 gsm.
Production: Cover: 5 colour plus Plastakoated outside.
Embossed by Avon Graphics.
Inside: 1 colour plus matt varnish.
Text: 28 pages: 4 colour process PMS Grey 6C. matt and gloss varnish wet on dry. 28 pages: 2 colours.
Press: Heidelberg Speedmaster 5 colour 40".

DESIGNER'S COMMENT
Elda Charous, Kameruka Design Group:

"The design brief was to announce the new Network TEN and the acquisition of talented production personnel, on-air personalities and programmes. This was partly achieved by the use of large bold photographs featuring those high profile personalities and quality programming.

During that year Network TEN created a new corporate identity and the cover was designed to supplant previous symbols and announce the commitment of Northern Star Holdings to Channel Ten and the electronic image."

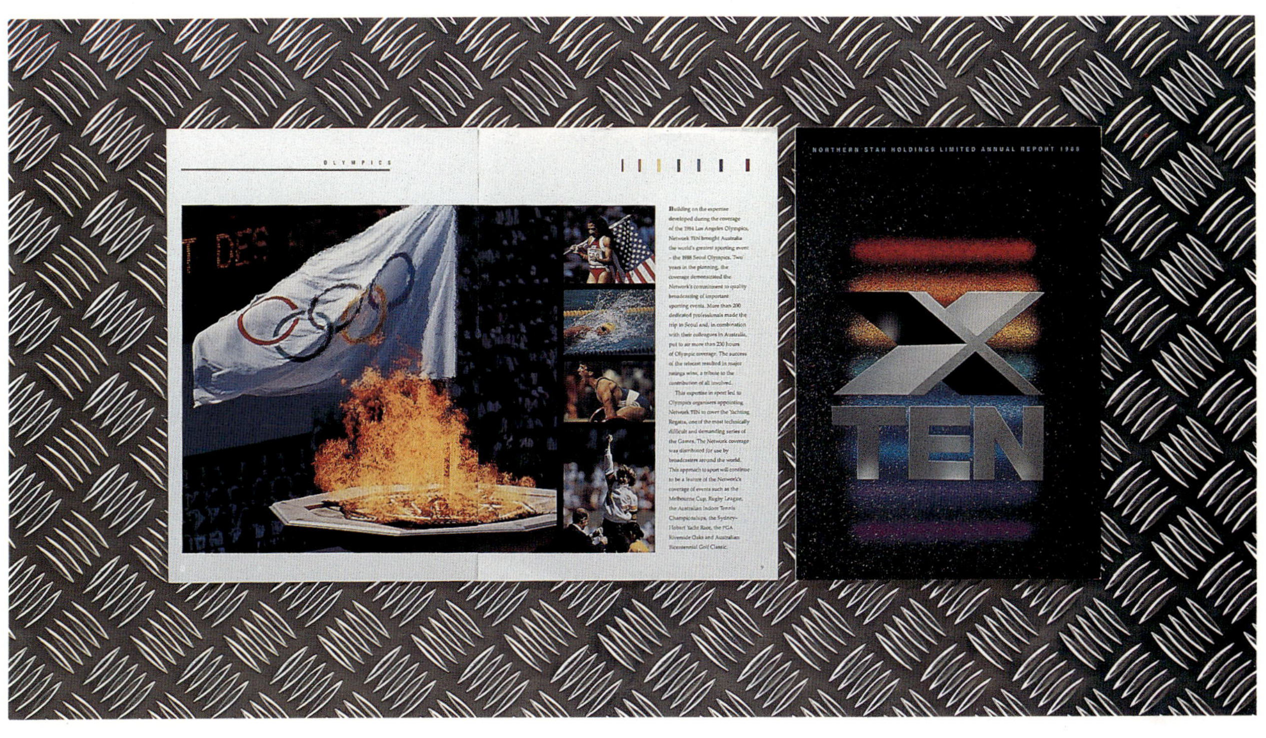

Designer: Elda Charous, Sydney.

QINTEX 1988 ANNUAL REPORT

Designer: Helen Kent, Melbourne.
Printer: Owen King Printers, Melbourne.
Paper: Cover: Tomasetti Mother of Pearl White Chromolux.
Text: Tomasetti White A Dull 170 gsm.
Production: Cover: 4 colour process. Foil stamped and embossed die-cut by Avon Graphics.
Text: 4 colour process, 1 PMS. Spot Gloss Varnish.
Press: Komori 6 colour 40″.

Designer: Helen Kent, Melbourne.

CAPEL COURT 1988 ANNUAL REPORT

Designer: Warwick Cruise Graphic Design, Melbourne.
Printer: Incolour Printing, Melbourne.
Paper: Cover: Tomasetti White A Artboard 310 gsm.
Flyleaf: Curtis Flannell Natural White.
Text: Tomasetti White A Dull 170 gsm.
Financial: Tomasetti Ikonorex Dull 150 gsm.
Producation: 4 colour process plus 1 special PMS.
Cover: Embossed plus foil stamped by Avon Graphics.
Press: Heidelberg Speedmaster 7V.

DESIGNER'S COMMENT

Warwick Cruise:

"This report was designed to emphasise the Client's decision to incorporate regional electronic media in its Corporate Finance Division's area of industry specialisation.

As a result, we designed a report with an Historical Essay of the media in Australia, running through it.

We believe the result was most interesting to users of the report, and the combination of historical photos, illustrations and advertisements, combined with modern photography worked extremely well."

Warwick Cruise Graphic Design, Melbourne.

WESTFIELD 1988 ANNUAL REPORT

Designer: Elda Charous (Kameruka), Sydney.
Printer: Southbank Printing Services, Melbourne.
Paper: Cover: Tomasetti White A Artboard 310 gsm.
Text: Tomasetti Ikonorex Dull Ivory 170 gsm.
Production: Cover: Printed 4 colour process plus 1 special, Plastakoated.
Inside: 2 colours.
Text: 24 pages, 4 colour process plus Cool Grey matt plus gloss varnish. Wet on dry.
Financial: 2 colours.
Cover: Embossed by Avon Graphics.

DESIGNER'S COMMENT

Elda Charous, Kameruka Design Group:

"Westfield International Inc. owns and manages seven regional shopping centres in the United States. Following significant success, this was the company's first annual report after only two months as an independent operator.

The design brief was to reflect the group's rapid success in the United States and confidence in the planned expansion to Europe.
An optimistic and interesting concept was required to support the available Westfield stock photographs.
By creating the transparent map and photographing it in three positions, it was possible to identify and locate the seven key properties and make a pictorial suggestion of the planned expansion into Europe. Extending the three dimensional theme, the graphs celebrate the company's excellent financial results."

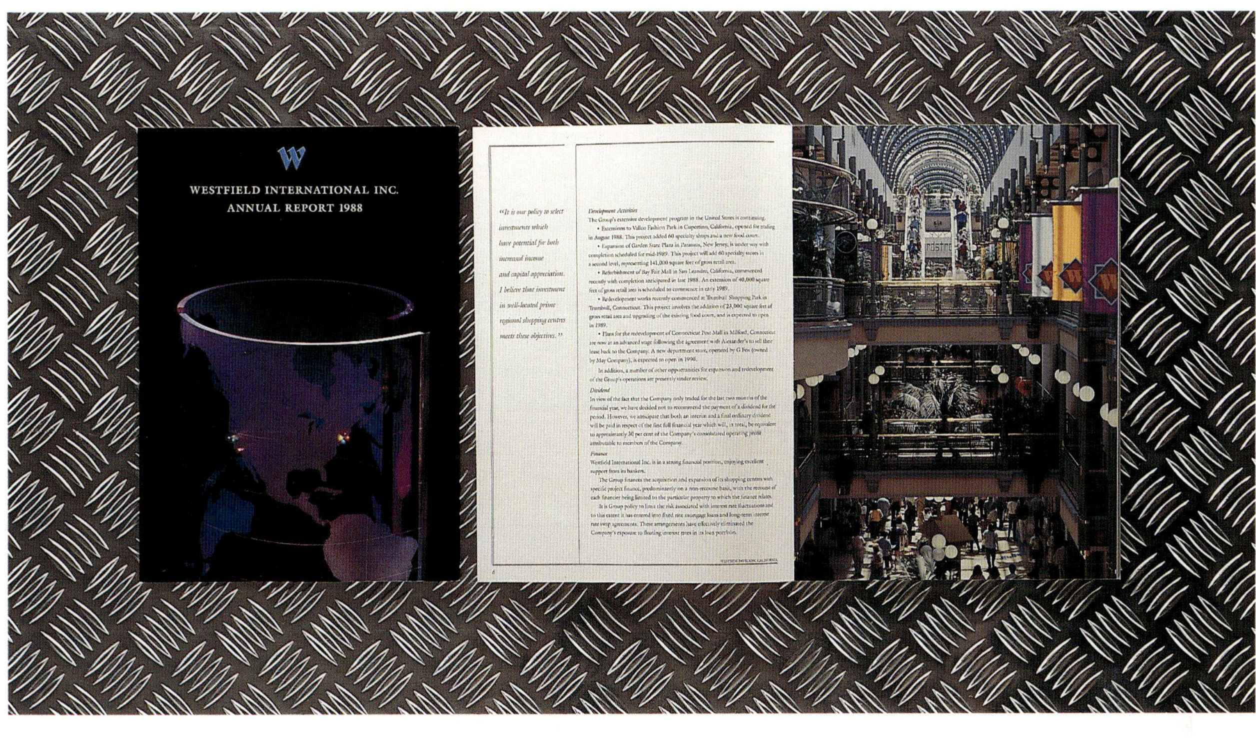

WESTFIELD INTERNATIONAL INC.
ANNUAL REPORT 1988

"It is our policy to select investments which have potential for both increased income and capital appreciation. I believe that investment in well-located prime regional shopping centres meets these objectives."

Development Activities
The Group's extensive development program in the United States is continuing.

• Extensions to Vallco Fashion Park in Cupertino, California, opened for trading in August 1988. This project added 60 specialty shops and a new food court.

• Expansion of Garden State Plaza in Paramus, New Jersey, is under way with completion scheduled for mid-1989. This project will add 60 specialty stores in a second level, representing 141,000 square feet of gross retail area.

• Refurbishment of Bay Fair Mall in San Leandro, California, commenced recently with completion anticipated in late 1988. An extension of 40,000 square feet of gross retail area is scheduled to commence in early 1989.

• Redevelopment works recently commenced at Trumbull Shopping Park in Trumbull, Connecticut. This project involves the addition of 23,000 square feet of gross retail area and upgrading of the existing food court, and is expected to open in 1989.

• Plans for the redevelopment of Connecticut Post Mall in Milford, Connecticut are now at an advanced stage following the agreement with Alexander's to sell their lease back to the Company. A new department store, operated by G Fox (owned by May Company), is expected to open in 1990.

In addition, a number of other opportunities for expansion and redevelopment of the Group's operations are presently under review.

Dividend
In view of the fact that the Company only traded for the last two months of the financial year, we have decided not to recommend the payment of a dividend for the period. However, we anticipate that both an interim and a final ordinary dividend will be paid in respect of the first full financial year which will, in total, be equivalent to approximately 30 per cent of the Company's consolidated operating profit attributable to members of the Company.

Finance
Westfield International Inc. is in a strong financial position, enjoying excellent support from its bankers.

The Group finances the acquisition and expansion of its shopping centres with specific project finance, predominantly on a non-recourse basis, with the recourse of each financier being limited to the particular property to which the finance relates.

It is Group policy to limit the risk associated with interest rate fluctuations and to this extent it has entered into fixed rate mortgage loans and long-term interest rate swap agreements. These arrangements have effectively eliminated the Company's exposure to floating interest rates in its loan portfolio.

Designer: Elda Charous, Sydney.

S.A. BREWING HOLDINGS LIMITED
1988 ANNUAL REPORT

Designer: A.D.S. Adelaide.
Printer: Consolidated Graphics, Adelaide.
Paper: Cover: Tomasetti White A Artboard 230 gsm.
Text: Tomasetti White A Dull 150 gsm.
Production: Cover: 4 colour process plus U.V. varnish. Embossed.
Text: 4 colour process.
Press: Heidelberg Speedmaster.

DESIGNER'S COMMENT
Ray Firth, designer/illustrator,
Advertising Design Studio, Adelaide:

"The report required the use of a geometrical abstract to attract attention to its dominating simplicity of shapes and sizes, so that the design not be compromised by the singular inference of the Company's activities which its name, SA Brewing Holdings, suggests.

By positioning the abstract design on the front cover in the same prominent place throughout the report, and the use of monotone pics to add depth and contrast, the torn-away effects revealed the diversity of the Company's operations."

Advertising Design Studio. Adelaide.

CBFC 1988 ANNUAL REPORT

Designer:	Corporate Graphics, Sydney.
Printer:	R. T. Kelly, Sydney.
Paper:	Cover: Tomasetti White A Artboard 260 gsm. Text: Tomasetti White A Dull 128 gsm.
Production:	Cover: 5 colour plus spot varnish outside. 2 colour plus spot varnish inside. Text: 4 colour process plus PMS 302, tinted and spot gloss varnish throughout. Press: Heidelberg Speedmaster 5 colour. Heidelberg SORM Z 2 colour.

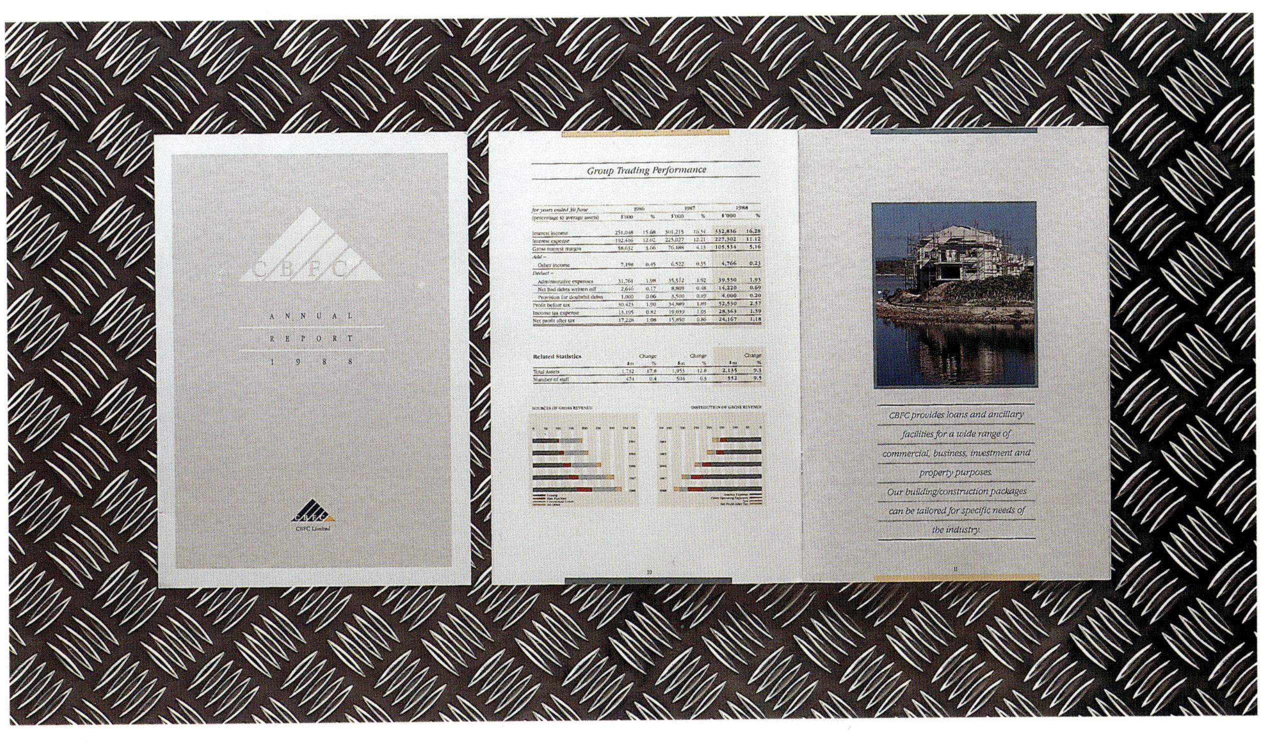

Corporate Graphics, Sydney (NLIE)

STATE BANK OF SOUTH AUSTRALIA
1989 ANNUAL REPORT

Designer: Charles Cannon Design, Adelaide.
Printer: Finsbury Press, Adelaide.
Photographer: Milton Wordley Associates, Adelaide.
Paper: Cover: Imperial Deluxe cover 256 gsm.
Text: Imperial Gloss 150 gsm.
Financial: Retreeve Earthtints 50% recycled 100 gsm.
Reproduction: (Film) Scantec, Adelaide.
Production: Cover: 4 colour process plasticoated.
Text: 4 colour process.
Financial: 1 colour.

DESIGNER'S COMMENT
Graham Pankhurst, Charles Cannon Design.

"At Charles Cannon Design, we believe the most important ingredients in producing an Annual Report are, a good client/production house relationship, a relevant theme, and good photography.

These three elements are clearly demonstrated in the State Bank's 1989 Annual Report.

In all phases of its production, from the initial concept stages to the printing, we worked in close co-operation with the Bank. This made for a free flow of communications, and a smooth production schedule.

The Report's theme was established very early, and ensured a continuity of style and direction. In this case, phrases from the Bank's Mission Statement we used as headings to establish philosophies for the various divisions of the bank.

Whether the often held view that "nobody reads annual reports" is true or not, we believe it is true that the photographs have the greatest initial impact. To this end we spent a great deal of time and effort in ensuring the photographs were just right".

Charles Cannon Design, Adelaide.

TRICONTINENTAL
1988 ANNUAL REPORT

Designer:	Daryl Turner Design, Melbourne.
Printer:	Owen King, Melbourne.
Paper:	Cover: Tomasetti Ikonorex Dull 300 gsm. Text: Tomasetti Ikonorex Dull 150 gsm.
Production:	Cover: 4 colour process. Hot foil Stamping. Die Cutting. Glueing plus matt celloglaze. Press: Heidelberg Speedmaster 4 colour 40″.

DESIGNER'S COMMENT
Daryl Turner:

"The Report was designed to highlight the breadth of companies that Tricontinental supported.

The brief stipulated a contemporary and forward looking approach. This was achieved by simple, clean typography and striking photography."

Daryl Turner Design, Melbourne.

ELDERS IXL 1988 ANNUAL REPORT

Designer: Emery Vincent Associates, Melbourne.
Printer: Canberra Press, Melbourne.
Paper: Cover: Tomasetti White A Artboard 310 gsm.
Text: Tomasetti White A Dull 150 gsm.
Production: Text: 4 colour process.
Matt Black. Spot gloss varnish.
Press: Komori 6 colour 40″.

DESIGNER'S COMMENT
Garry Emery, Emery Vincent Associates:

"The cover of the Annual Report summarises the company's major businesses and is a response to the Chairman's direction that each major business be equally represented in a simple, direct graphic communication.

The report reflects a 'no-nonsense' approach to business and displays primary photographic colour images superimposed with secondary graphic product and services references.

The financial information component of the report was produced economically, separately bound and inserted into a folded extension to the back cover."

Emery Vincent Associates, Melbourne.

QUEENSLAND AUSTRALIA PROFILE

Designer: Rankin Design Group, Melbourne.
Printer: Prestige Litho, Brisbane.
Paper: Cover: Tomasetti White A Artboard 310 gsm.
Text: Tomasetti White A Dull 128 gsm.
Production: 4 colour process plus gloss varnish.

DESIGNER'S COMMENT

"The book was designed to be a colourful, friendly document reflecting the atmosphere and excitement of the State and the warmth of its people. We were determined it should not be seen as just another conventional, government-style publication.

The choice of photographs was of primary concern and the designer spent considerable time in Brisbane personally selecting shots from the government photographic library."

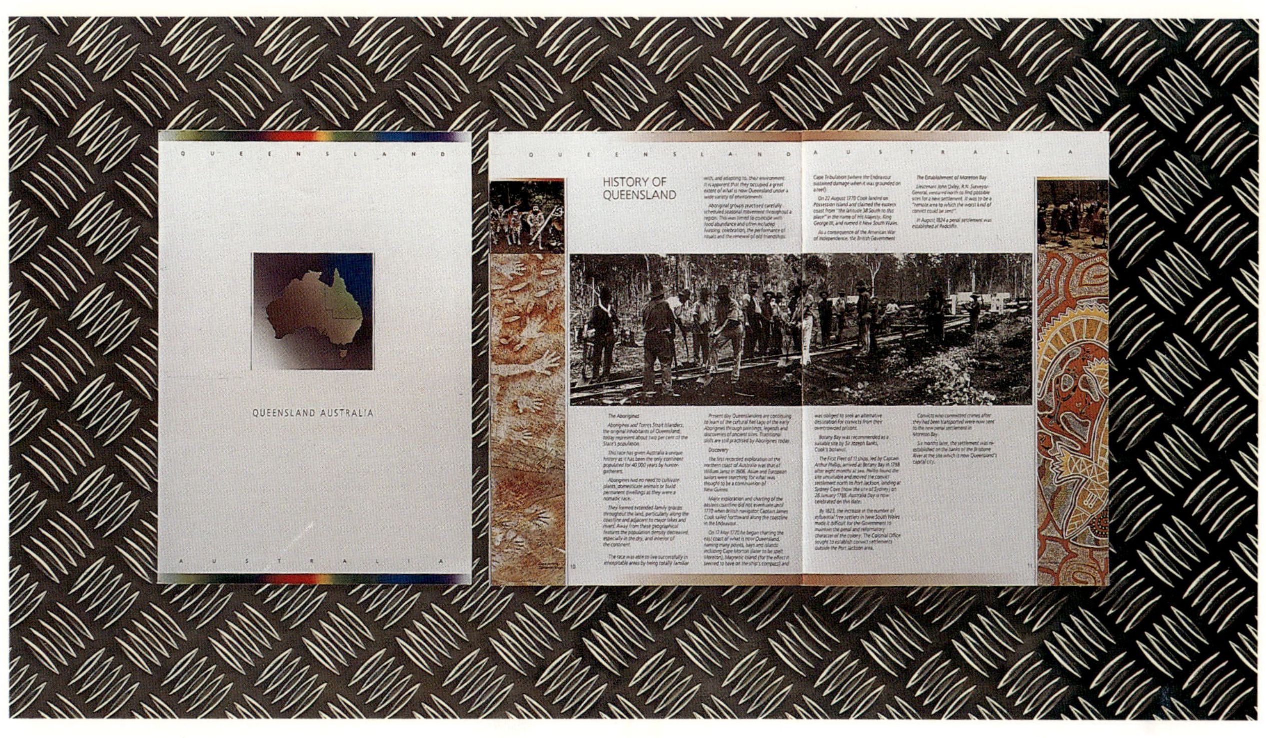

Rankin Design Group, Melbourne.

GREEN PAGES.

PHOTOGRAPHERS: NEW SOUTH WALES

Paul Able (02) 439 8730
Peter Adams (02) 99 4429
John Adams (02) 699 8099
Christopher Adams (02) 919 5836
Bruce Alexander (02) 955 6789
Brett Allat (02) 319 2511
Alvarez (02) 357 1488
Geoff Ambler (02) 810 7994
Mark Amos (02) 437 4424
J. Barry Anderson (02) 326 1182
Michael Andrews (02) 949 6815
Mark Anthony (02) 437 5555
Howard Archbold (02) 438 4695
Bob Armstrong (02) 922 4200
Keith Arnold (02) 810 6786
James Ashburn (02) 955 8598
David Austen (02) 957 2511
Paul Austin (02) 437 5555
Quentin Bacon (02) 99 2183
Jon Bader (02) 955 8110
Bruce Ballard (02) 436 3133
Ashley Barber (02) 516 3193
John Barrett (02) 810 2601
Tim Bauer (02) 281 4737
Phillip Baxter (02) 436 1908
Rodney Bayer (02) 319 2511
Derek Bierman (02) 212 5799
Robert Billington (02) 419 3402
Patrick Bingham-Hall (02) 29 7910
Brian Bird (02) 319 2511
Geoffrey Brawn (02) 955 4399
Geoff Brown (02) 818 5644. Page 26
Jim Brownett (02) 683 6433
Andrew Brucker (02) 357 1488
Urs Buhlman (02) 955 5845
David Buley (02) 371 9565
Carsten Burmeister (02) 955 8110
Peter Caine (02) 906 2330
John Callanan (02) 92 7158
Scott Cameron (02) 952 2712
Barry Campbell (02) 959 5713
Kraig Carlstrom (02) 954 4315
Tony Carpenter (02) 438 3428
Philip Castleton (02) 818 5644
Russell Chant (02) 516 5011
Michael Chittenden (02) 698 8207
David Chivers (02) 319 1877
Paul Clarke (02) 211 0514
John Clutterbuck (02) 909 2594
Brett Cochrane (02) 318 1281
Gerald Colley (02) 922 1077
Tim Collis-Bird (02) 419 8158
Peter Colville (02) 922 1077
Stak Contantinou (02) 953 8283
Michael Cook (02) 699 3981
Mark Crawford (02) 699 7548
Peter Crawford (02) 981 1462
Vivienne Cray (02) 958 2875
Stuart Crossett (02) 810 6555
Craig Cumming (02) 332 2100
David Cumming (02) 810 7044
John Curnow (02) 692 9966
Trevern Dawes (02) 638 6995
Christina De Water (02) 30 1737
James Domingo (02) 699 4303
Ken Duncan (043) 84 6275
Neil Duncan (02) 50 6359
Ron Dunphy (02) 919 5099
Gary Ede (02) 427 6182
Sandy Edwards (02) 698 7463
Chad Ehlers (02) 555 7449
Chris Elfes (02) 529 4699
Mike Elton (02) 449 5937
Robert Erdmann (02) 357 1488
Per Ericson (02) 555 2600
George Farrell (02) 437 5555
Philip Fischer (02) 319 1877
Gerrit Fokkema (02) 569 8496
Rowan Fotheringham (02) 818 1466
David Franklin (02) 957 1829
Ron Freer (02) 77 8410
Robert Fretwell (02) 716 6434. Page 32
Brian Furley (02) 747 4768
Andrew Gardner (02) 953 8400
John Garth (02) 439 7116
Brian Gatenby (02) 955 6789
Richard Gates (02) 332 2100
Bernie Gibson (02) 922 4607
Graeme Gillies (02) 906 1167
Nicholas Gleitzman (02) 810 2601
Richard Glover (02) 319 1877
Walter Glover (02) 660 5807
Serge Golikov (02) 858 4149
Philip Gray (02) 958 0092
Ross Gray (02) 439 6739
Gary Grealy (02) 922 2712
Tony Gunn (02) 963 2239
David Haddon (02) 517 2626
Phil Haley (02) 438 4773
Greg Hard (02) 818 5644
Brad Harris (02) 550 9211
Simon Harsent (02) 318 1281
Brian Hart (02) 449 4689
Scott Hawkins (02) 517 2626
Phillip Hayson (02) 968 1985
Rob Henderson (02) 922 1103
Peter Henning (02) 981 5189
Mark Herron (02) 954 4670
Jon Higgs (02) 922 6933
Brett Hilder (02) 331 5563
Brian Hinder (02) 660 5530
John Hiscock (02) 550 4233
Tim Hixson (02) 922 2712
Robin Hodgkinson (02) 698 8207
Wayne Holloway (02) 550 3730
Ross Honeysett (02) 361 6650
Horizon (02) 957 5412
Hot Shots (02) 671 2244
Julie Howard (02) 818 5644
Imagewide (02) 365 0844
Ray Jarratt (02) 319 1877
Carolyn Johns (02) 30 1737
Peter Johnson (02) 211 2854
Errol Jones (02) 939 7066
Howard Jones (02) 699 9103
Patrick Jones (02) 331 2044
Ron Jones (02) 954 9303
Clive Kane (02) 922 3111
David Kay (02) 818 5644
Bob King (02) 818 5644
Konrad (02) 922 6933
Mark Lang (02) 30 1737
Michael Langford (02) 698 8207
James Latter (02) 959 5144
Leighton Studios (02) 319 2511
Dan Lepart (02) 357 1488
David Liddle (02) 810 8552
Rob Little (02) 212 6962
Mark Llewellynn (02) 810 2601. Page 28
Ellio Loccisano (02) 30 8089
Jon Love (02) 699 2318
Ian Lovegreen (02) 981 1428
Stephen Lowe (02) 516 5011
Geoff Lung (02) 331 1922
Mike Lyon (02) 357 6707
Tony Lyon (02) 331 5675
Ashley Mackevicius (02) 810 2601
Warren Macris (02) 579 5556
Sten Magnussen (02) 498 6289
Christopher Mann (02) 689 2555
Roger Marchant (02) 389 9816
John Marmaras (02) 387 5363
Grant Matthews (02) 357 1488
Graham McCarter (02) 810 2961
Brian McInerney (02) 922 3847
Peter McIntosh (02) 922 1077
Matthew McKie (02) 698 8207
Jack Meagher (02) 360 3927
Brent Melton (02) 389 4865
Wayne Miles (02) 810 7921
Dave Miller (02) 698 9281
Leon Mills (02) 569 1906
Bob Mitchell (02) 281 6342
Graham Monro (02) 555 1828
Robert Monro (02) 550 9211
David Moore (02) 30 1737
Robert Morehead (02) 922 2712
Lewis Morley (02) 211 2002
Lance Nelson (02) 331 1663
Paul Nevin (02) 692 9966
Robbi Newman (02) 955 7150
Vantuan Nguyen (02) 411 7771
Michael Nicholson (02) 436 4939
Richie Nicholson (02) 906 1877
Jeff Nield (02) 439 2700
Warren Norris (02) 449 4951
Maurice O'Connell (02) 438 4515
Michael Oakley (02) 212 6185
Margaret Olah (02) 555 1285
Lennart Osbeck (02) 957 6595
Lindsay Osborne (02) 212 6560
Greg Parsons (02) 810 6786
John Pateman (02) 955 7665
Andrew Payne (02) 818 4398
Richard Peake (02) 699 4514
Karl Peter-Gottschalk (02) 282 2012
Chris Pilz (02) 969 4213
Ian Potter (02) 959 4686
Pro-Image (02) 319 1877
Philip Quirk (02) 30 1737
Jeff Rand (02) 331 3154
Rapport (02) 698 8207
Willem Rethmeier (02) 281 1558
Brian Roberts (047) 57 1004
Tim Robinson (02) 331 2044
Gilbert Rossi (02) 818 2669
Tracy Rowe (02) 550 9211
Tandy Rowley (02) 331 2854
Jurgen Ryck (02) 212 4954
Jim Saliba (02) 481 0095
James Scanlon (02) 922 3004
Jacek Schilbach (02) 957 5633
George Seper (02) 211 4358

Chris Shain (02) 810 7775
Vikkj Skaratt (02) 331 2044
Michael Skelton (02) 810 6555
Greg Slater (02) 332 2100
Peter Sledge (02) 438 5651
Louis Smit (02) 516 5011
Heide Smith (062) 80 5430
Peter Smith (02) 451 8211
Sowerbv Smith (02) 922 2256
Lynne Smyth (02) 958 0016
Peter Solness (02) 30 1737
Veneslav Stanuga (02) 360 3927
Jacque Stevenson (02) 810 6555
Stock Shots (02) 810 7921. Page 26
Oliver Strewe (02) 30 1737
Sue Stubbs (02) 332 2100
North Sullivan (02) 212 5349
Duncan Taylor (02) 809 4345
Jim Townley (02) 957 6319
Robert Tuckwell (02) 698 8207
Grenville Turner (02) 30 1737
George Turton (02) 798 4731
Murray VanDanVeer (02) 550 2600
Malcolm Vaughan (02) 888 3764
Alan Vertue (02) 398 5475
Kurt Vollmer (02) 692 9966
Jon Waddy (02) 699 4514
Rob Walls (02) 698 8207
Andrew Warn (02) 955 4399
Julian Watt (02) 550 9211
Peter Webb (02) 698 7327
John Webber (02) 33 4592
Philip Weir (02) 438 4215
Tim Wheeler (02) 906 3133
Ken Wilde (02) 319 2511
Desmond Williams (02) 430 1606
Peter Wilkie (02) 660 4509
Mark Wilson (02) 211 0514
Andre Wohler (02) 437 5555
Billy Wrencher (02) 969 3825
XYZ (02) 212 5349
David Young (02) 555 1401
Vivian Zink (02) 818 5625

PHOTOGRAPHERS: QUEENSLAND
Agency Photographics (07) 343 3403
Tom Anthony (075) 382 2766
Paul Arrowsmith (07) 854 1708
Peter Budd (07) 391 6211
Mark Burgin (07) 369 6363
Andrew Campbell (07) 254 1110
Paul Candlin (07) 369 9735
Merv Cannon (07) 252 3511
Bryan Chester (07) 870 2795
Ron Cottee (07) 252 2099
John Dick (07) 252 2894
Chris Ellis (07) 369 6363
Karl Fehr (075) 30 5239
Derrick George (07) 252 4409
Ian Golding (07) 366 2681
Robert Gray (070) 52 1055
Barry Green (07) 252 2132
Jon Haigh (07) 369 5107
Mike Hallson (07) 358 3966
Brian Hand (07) 854 1708
Terry Hegerty (07) 394 4011
Andrew Houkamau (07) 391 6922
Stefan Jannides (07) 252 2943
Kingsridge (07) 208 8694
David Knell (07) 65 2277
Narelle Kremmer (07) 369 6363
Stephen Liddle (07) 207 5424
Rob Maccoll (07) 378 5332
David McCarthy (07) 891 1222. Page 38, 39
Peter Mylonas (07) 391 6922
Stephen Nutt (07) 822 1295
Kim Osborne (070) 98 6126
Bruce Peebles (07) 846 2550
Ian Poole (07) 831 4956
Craig Ratcliffe (07) 262 4572
Ron Ratcliffe (07) 262 4572
David Sandison (07) 839 3040
Marian See (07) 891 5466
Gary Sheppard (07) 391 6922
Michel Stasse (07) 844 9074
Russell Stokes (07) 252 7916
Terry Straight (07) 391 6211
Stephen Tierney (07) 854 1572
John Trost (070) 53 2962. Page 223
Eric Victor-Perdraut (07) 369 6363
Craig Veovodin (07) 368 2901
Tony Waller (07) 391 6922
Glenn Weiss (07) 252 9910
Greg Wilson (07) 857 1898

PHOTOGRAPHERS: NORTHERN TERRITORY
Barry Allwright (089) 52 1726
J Boutcher (089) 81 1553
John Butcher (089) 81 2516
David Haigh (089) 53 0255
David Hancock (089) 45 0052
Daniel Healy (089) 81 0361
Image Photographic (089) 81 8361
Imitrans (089) 53 0225
Peter Jarver (089) 81 6541
Nigel Jefford (089) 52 7272
Manfred Karlhuber (089) 81 7127
Ginette Kenney (089) 45 0052
Mirage (089) 53 0077
Denis O'Byrne (089) 52 1173
Outback Photographics (089) 52 3559
Palm Photographics (089) 81 6649
Silva (089) 41 0348
Steve Strike (089) 52 3559
Territory Photosport (089) 81 9733
Thunderhead (089) 81 6541

PHOTOGRAPHERS: SOUTH AUSTRALIA
Eric Algra (08) 224 0113
Annatone Studio (08) 49 7538
Argus IV (08) 340 1776
Philip Astley (08) 338 2655
James Bateman (08) 362 5965
Steve Berekmeri (08) 353 5754
Clive Birch (08) 271 9517
Don Brice (08) 231 0155
Marcus Brownrigg (08) 339 4711
Julie Byron (08) 333 0500
Mike Connell (08) 31 0000
Dieter Eubel (08) 46 0999
Peter Fisher (08) 231 0155
Trevor Fox (08) 338 2655
John Gitsham (08) 224 0818
Vic Grimmett (08) 293 4600
Grant Hancock (08) 271 1844
Stephen Hardacre (08) 221 1355
John Hemmings (08) 46 0999
Ashley Holmes (08) 353 2775
Richard Humphries (08) 231 0155
Imaginaction (08) 212 6175
Jag Photographics (08) 231 0018
Kevin Killey (08) 223 5300
Leawarra (08) 362 7981
Drew Lenman (08) 31 0000
Philip Martin (08) 46 0999
Clayton McWhinney (08) 338 2655
James Nicholson (08) 224 0818
Kevin O'Daly (08) 224 0113. Page 22, 23
Peter Schwarz (08) 271 1588
Lyndon Stacy (08) 271 1844
Bernd Stoecker (08) 278 2644
Bernard Van Elsen (08) 362 1977
Fergie Veitch (08) 362 1977
Peter Watkins (08) 338 2655
Ross Williams (08) 223 1242
Milton Wordley (08) 231 0155

PHOTOGRAPHERS: TASMANIA
Gary Alan (002) 72 5876
Richard Bennett (002) 97 1371
Steve Chika (002) 34 8139
Peter Clarkson (002) 31 0670
Concept Photographics (002) 23 4435
Richard Eastwood (002) 23 3839
Steve French (003) 34 1120
Paul Griggs (004) 24 6969
Owen Hughes (003) 31 1481
Ben Huisman (004) 29 1292
Steve Lovegrove (002) 24 0614
Magnum Photographics (002) 34 8139
Q Photographics (002) 31 2250
Verne Reid (002) 23 4271
Noeline Robinson (002) 23 3409
W. Penry Saward (003) 31 9702
Mark Seaton (004) 27 9117
John Thorp (003) 34 0909
Mark Tripp (003) 44 3439
Geoff Wharton (002) 61 1422
Colin Winter (004) 31 2755

PHOTOGRAPHERS: VICTORIA
Kelvin Aitken (03) 51 8761
A.G. Photography (03) 338 3664
Peter Akbiyik (03) 534 8144
Rick Altman (057) 8 2305. Page 24
Tony Amos (03) 521 3191
Neale Anderson (03) 529 2388
Rob Anderson (03) 824 2580
George Apostolidis (03) 826 3555
Mark Ashkanasy (03) 819 3141
A.S.P. Photography (03) 560 4974
Mal Austin (03) 793 2158
Bill Bachman (03) 882 2461
John Baghel (03) 241 4951
Peter Bailey (03) 241 7461
Andrew Baker (03) 878 1918
David Baker (03) 743 2473
Bill Baker (03) 699 4000
Geoffrey Baker (03) 890 3645
Kim Baker (03) 699 8786
John Banagan (03) 534 5502
Robert Banks (03) 329 2344
Graham Baring (03) 482 1708
Paul Barker (03) 882 8191

Rod Barkly (03) 529 4900
Peter Barr (03) 67 6338
Ross Barrett (03) 719 7245
Alex Bauer (03) 51 4122
Bayswater Commercial (03) 729 1180
John Beale (03) 241 5000
Tom Berry (03) 699 9699
Phillip Betts (03) 51 8761
Ross Bird (03) 534 8144
Graeme Black (03) 428 2739
Robert Blackburn (03) 328 2120
John Bodin (03) 51 9932
Terence Bogue (03) 417 1005
John Bolton (03) 51 6987
BonneyLeder (03) 882 4046
Brian Brandt (03) 51 9932
Sean Brandt (03) 52 9932
John Brash (03) 67 6338
John Brown (03) 347 7982
Christopher Budgeon (03) 827 6663
James Byron (03) 529 5480
Doug Campbell (03) 529 2144
Darren Capp (03) 645 2635
Bruce Carr (03) 699 8450
Earl Carter (03) 51 4887
Murray Case (03) 645 2316
Kevin Cassidy (03) 699 4000
Stan Cesnik (03) 240 0044
Peter Champion (03) 509 5347. Page 30
Paul Child (03) 826 3555
Christo (03) 419 3874
Monty Coles (03) 267 4005
David Cook (03) 571 9233
Mary Cooke (03) 699 9699
Michael Corridore (03) 699 9699
Coventry Studios (03) 699 9622
Michael Coyne (03) 489 8435
Lynton Crabb (03) 525 3408
Robert Cracknell (03) 482 1480
Andrew Craig (03) 699 9699
Lou D'Angelo (03) 827 6663
Steve Darby (03) 521 2216
Kerrie Day (03) 645 2316
Aran De Bruijn (03) 763 4393
Rick De Carteret (03) 531 6933
Tim DeNeefe (03) 328 4037
Heather Dinas (03) 240 0044
Roger Du Buisson (03) 699 7600
Mike Dunn (03) 240 0044
Peter Dunphy (03) 696 5144
Gary Edwards (03) 529 8736
Rennie Ellis (03) 521 2233
Rudi Everts (03) 529 2226
Tony Fagioli (03) 824 2059
Graeme Farr (03) 240 0044
Heather Favel (03) 531 1335
Alan Fawcett (03) 481 4040
Tony Feder (03) 329 2344
Mike Fisher (03) 543 2295
Eryk Fitzkau (03) 837 5397
Peter Flight (03) 347 7882
Terry Forrester (03) 380 1523
Terry Foster (03) 509 4353
Simon Frith (03) 529 4900
Eddie Gaber (03) 699 2444
Nick Galanos (03) 529 4900
John Ganci (03) 826 3324
Andrew Gash (03) 51 9932

Gasworks (03) 426 1444
Arthur George (03) 329 1777
Brian Gilkes (03) 329 1777
Paul Glasser (03) 328 4037
Patrick Goggins (03) 486 6544
John Gollings (03) 428 4399
Kate Gollings (03) 419 7619
Sebastion Gollings (03) 428 4399
Peter Gough (03) 6991519
Roger Gould (03) 690 6011
Chiara Goya (03) 347 5768
Regina Grant (03) 690 7820
Tim Greig (03) 525 3408
Tim Griffith (03) 689 6771
George Haig (03) 699 8786
Wes Halloran (03) 645 2625
Mark Hancock (03) 529 4900
Mark Harper (03) 824 0955
John Hay (03) 882 6870
Angie Heinl (03) 826 3555
Peter Hendrie (03) 699 7833
Jacqui Henshaw (03) 883 0252
Rob Hickman (03) 531 5365
Paul Hicks (03) 241 6511
Frank Hoekstra (03) 529 6282
Ron Hood (03) 699 8508
Jim Hooper (03) 489 5443
Les Horvat (03) 529 2144
Graham Hosking (03) 529 4900
Peter Houghton (03) 690 7711
Dominic Hsieh (03) 826 3555
John Humphrey (03) 5251690
Peter Hyatt (03) 3291777
Rob Imhoff (03) 529 2144
Impressions (03) 329 2344
Chris Ioannou (03) 328 4037
Tania Janovich (03) 328 2120
Peter Johnson (03) 211 8608
Ashley Jones Evans (03) 826 3555
Rhonda Joyce (03) 531 8293
Ted Keogh (03) 529 2877
John Kirby (03) 645 2071
Ted Klosynski (03) 670 6338
Demetre Kodellas (03) 521 2672
Philip Korczynski (03) 529 2226
John Krutop (03) 329 2344
Doug Lacey (03) 699 8834
Jean-Marc La Roque (03) 509 3453
Guy Lamothe (03) 690 2831
Latrobe Studios (03) 699 2444
Michael Laurie (03) 690 2525
James Lauritz (03) 646 1111
Rob Lawler (03) 699 9826
Peter Leaver (03) 51 8761
Antony Leong (03) 328 3937
Alan Louey (03) 51 6987
Neil Lorimer (03) 251 5479
Robin Lowe (03) 497 1322
Ern Mainka (03) 241 2994
Nigel Malone (03) 650 6339
Earl Mant (03) 699 8786
Shane Martin (03) 426 1444
Tony Masci (03) 529 8736
Arthur Massey (03) 583 8065
Pierre Mathison (03) 824 0955
Paul Matthews (03) 670 6338
James McFarlane (03) 529 4900
Ian McKenzie (03) 329 1777

Trevor Mein (03) 528 1395
David Meldrum (03) 241 5000
Gerhardt Mertens (03) 696 4478
Richard Millott (03) 534 0568
Garry Moore (03) 240 0044
Geoff Moorfoot (03) 818 3301
Tony Moran (03) 699 2444
Alan Morgans (03) 419 4686
Dieter Muller (03) 690 2774
Robin Myers (03) 699 8450
Nadish Naoroji (03) 509 1331
Rick Nastovski (03) 583 0553
Graeme Neander (03) 699 9622
Frank Neilsen (03) 885 4391
Graham Nicholson (03) 534 0568
Simon Obarzanek (03) 645 2316
John O'Flaherty (03) 523 0955
John Ogden (03) 570 6547
John Palermo (03) 883 5286
Chris Parks (03) 529 8008
Sally Ann Pascoe (03) 699 9699
Paul Perillo (03) 419 4466
Michael Perry (03) 690 4066
Louis Petruccelli (03) 521 1220
Bernie Phelan (03) 51 8022
Mauro Pomponio (03) 537 2265
Bob Purvis (03) 660 2240
Nicholas Quin (03) 836 0914
Mark Rayner (03) 818 3301
Ken Redpath (03) 589 5766
Hank Rem (03) 529 6282
Sal Ricca (03) 696 2787
Robert Rice (03) 241 8154
Michael Richards (03) 521 2216
Bernie Richter (052) 63 2425
Maurice Rinaldi (03) 417 6849
Otto Rogge (03) 859 3157
Mannix Rousseau (03) 696 4966
Ken Runtuwene (03) 428 4399
Peter Russell (03) 529 8736
Mike Rutherford (03) 428 4399
Denis Ryan (03) 690 8039
Donna Ryder (03) 531 1335
Tony Sanders (03) 529 8736
Ezio Sanelli (03) 51 8049
Emmanuel Santos (03) 328 2120
Jack Sarafian (03) 696 3660
Paul Saville (03) 699 7603
David Scaletti (03) 347 4005
Pat Scanlon (03) 482 3669
Paul Scott (03) 534 0568
Chris Shields (03) 645 2280
Wolfgang Sievers (03) 598 4602
Tomek Sikora (03) 827 5397. Page 40
David Simmonds (03) 690 5176
Martin Simons (03) 525 3979
Maxine Sims (059) 75 8286
Alan Sinden (03) 645 2280
Bill Skajec (03) 645 2625
Garry Smith (03) 699 2444
Rob Spaulding (03) 571 9233
Paul Steel (03) 531 4316
John Street (03) 699 8484
Studio One (03) 553 1077
Peter Suveges (03) 696 4900
Peter Swan (03) 529 2929
Andy Tavares (03) 426 1444
Leanne Temme (03) 690 7711

Giles Terrier (03) 529 4900
Laurie Thomas (03) 386 6289
Peter Thomson (03) 529 2388
Tomek & Eryk (03) 827 5397. Page 40
Ross Tonkin (03) 690 4066
Paul Torcello (03) 529 2144
Paul Tremelling (03) 529 2155
Steve Tunaley-Assist. (03) 861 5622
Bernard Van de Geer (03) 699 4495
Gus Van Der Heyde (03) 660 2244
Tony Vandenburg (03) 529 6566
Adrian Van Valen (03) 696 5988
Patrick Varney (03) 699 9622
Paul Velissaris (03) 240 8065
Lupco Veljanovski (03) 696 8141
David Verrall (03) 531 3355
Phillip Virgo (03) 509 5347
Robert Vitale (03) 240 8065
Joe Vittorio (03) 529 2144. Page 20
James Vlahogiannis (018) 338 800
Tom Vonertzen (03) 296 1465
Peter Vorlicek (03) 51 5010
Andrew Vukasov (03) 883 5156
Peter Wakeman (03) 699 1647
Rick Wallis (03) 241 5000
James Walshe (03) 347 4005
Bruce Walter (03) 419 4686
Peter Walton (03) 848 9932. Page 34
Bob Watson (03) 426 1444
Kevan Way (03) 328 4812
Graeme Webber (03) 429 4147
Michael Wennrich (03) 660 2240
James Widdowson (03) 699 5507
John Williams (03) 824 1101
Norman Wodetski (03) 328 1142
Bill Wright (03) 347 4922
Gavin Wright (03) 532 0505
Philip Wymant (03) 699 2444
Tat Ming Yu (03) 240 0044
Lynette Zeeng (03) 51 8761

PHOTOGRAPHERS: WESTERN AUSTRALIA
Errol Bartlett (09) 274 6528
Trevor Bennett (09) 447 3510
Leon Bird (09) 444 7971
Brigitte Braun (09) 384 1980
John Bruin (09) 324 1929
Graeme Collopy (09) 401 3659
Angus Colquohoun (09) 328 3656
Michael Coupe (09) 271 9344
Simon Cowling (09) 430 4929
Bill Crabb (09) 387 5783
David Dare Parker (09) 444 5893
David Davies (09) 385 1927
Ashley De Prazer (09) 321 4291
Jeremy Dixon-Peters (09) 328 5144
Greg Edwards (09) 322 1941
Phil England (09) 221 1249
Fab (09) 388 2144
Geoff Fisher (09) 383 3898
Fotocol (09) 387 1461
Richard Gale (09) 388 2144
Peter Garside (09) 328 1977
Robert Garvey (09) 446 9228
Roger Garwood (09) 335 1063
Fiona Girvan-Brown (09) 361 4999
Keith Gottschalk (09) 362 2072
Chris Ha (09) 344 8878
Bob Hannan (09) 321 2364
Tony Harrison (09) 328 8589
Murray Hennessey (09) 328 4994
Greg Hocking (09) 388 2938
Noel Holly (09) 322 1494
David Irvin (09) 381 6033
Michael James (09) 443 1775
Will Kohlen (09) 361 3720
Fritz Kos (09) 328 5076
Andrew Lastman (09) 249 1816
Max Lawrence (09) 444 1177
Roel Loopers (09) 384 1980
Con Macarlino (09) 382 1422
Bruce Maconochie (09) 332 5354
Keith Francis Marks (09) 272 4850
Kim Martin (09) 401 5020
Geoffrey McKell (09) 388 2090
Richard Meyers (09) 324 1050
Tris Milburn (09) 274 6528
Felicity Morel (09) 328 8589
Graeme Noack (09) 388 4466
A.J. Nutt (09) 325 3607
Ocean Photos (09) 401 5020
Geoff Osborne (09) 388 1078
Tom Pomnay (09) 387 1461
Rapport (09) 430 4929
Raymond Ratcliffe (09) 328 2203
Ewan Robinson (09) 388 4466
Bill Rose (09) 388 2938
Bob Sach (09) 367 6095
Garry Sarre (09) 227 8197
Klaus Schmechtig (09) 450 3378
Louise Scott (09) 480 4639
Ian Seargeant (09) 388 2144
Murray Simon (09) 227 6372
Shirley Slater (09) 322 7531
Brian Stevenson (09) 362 3044
Don Stevenson (09) 325 3607
Ron Tan (09) 277 8197
Leon Tang (09) 328 2198
Lynne Taylor Rennie (09) 328 4994
Simon Westlake (09) 322 1494
Nicholas White (09) 277 8711
John Whitfield-King (09) 361 9054
Barry Williams (09) 388 2626
Dirk Wittenberg (09) 293 1674
Richard Woldendorp (09) 481 0375
Bruno Zimmerman (09) 272 3622

PHOTO LIBRARIES: NEW SOUTH WALES
ABC Stock Shot Library (02) 437 8070
Auscape International (02) 698 5455
Austral-International (02) 439 8222
Australian Picture Library (02) 438 3011
Australian Transparencies Library (02) 358 2094
Baglin Douglass (02) 437 6311
Bay Picture Library (02) 662 8777
Colour Australia (02) 326 2989
Dive 2000 (02) 90 7783
Film Australia Footage (02) 467 9777
Horizon International (02) 957 5412
Image Bank (02) 922 6373
International Photographic Library (02) 920 5008
Ken Duncan Australia Wide (043) 67 6777
Mitchell Picture Collection (02) 230 1414
Photo Library of Australia (02) 929 8511
Rapport Photo Agency (02) 698 8207
Richcolour China pics (02) 489 3078
Sea Australia Resource Centre (02) 525 1426
Sportshoot (02) 451 8040
Sportshots (02) 663 2843
Stills Stock (02) 939 7066
Stock Shots (02) 818 5644. Page 26, 27
Tony Stone Worldwide (02) 929 8511
Welldon Trannies (02) 955 1140
Wildlight Photo Agency (02) 30 1737

PHOTO LIBRARIES: NORTHERN TERRITORY
Backgrounds (089) 81 6541
Hancock & Kenney (089) 45 0052
Mirage (089) 53 0077
Outback Photographics (089) 52 2088
Silva (089) 41 0348
Territory Photosport (089) 81 9733

PHOTO LIBRARIES: QUEENSLAND
Dept Env. & Heritage Photo Library (07) 227 6123
Positive Image Photo Library (07) 252 2894
Queensland Tourist and TravelCorp (07) 833 5400
Sea Australia Resource Centre (07) 341 8931
Stills (07) 262 7355
Tropics Photomedia (070) 53 2962

PHOTO LIBRARIES: SOUTH AUSTRALIA
Oz Image (08) 270 3009
International Photo Library (08) 250 2201
Lotsa Shots (08) 239 0488
Pasquale Giorgio (08) 340 0961
Photo Flinders (08) 269 7455
Steve Berekmeri (08) 353 5754

PHOTO LIBRARY: TASMANIA
Q. Photographics (002) 31 2250

PHOTOGRAPHIC LIBRARIES: VICTORIA
ABC Stock Shot Library (03) 524 2278
All Sport (03) 690 6011
Alpine Images (03) 819 3141
Andrew Baker Photo Library (03) 878 1918
Auschromes (03) 699 3222. Page 228, 229
Australasian Nature Transparencies (03) 458 4591
Cooee Historical Picture Library (03) 531 6375
Cooee Picture Library (03) 531 6876
Glamabank (03) 489 6544
I.L.A. Photo Library (03) 885 1547
Image Bank (03) 699 7833
Images Worldwide (03) 378 9404
Impressions Photo Sports Library (03) 329 2344
International Photo Library (03) 521 1716
Jacqui Mott Photo Search (03) 689 2448
Jennifer Richardson Photo Library (03) 762 7018
Ken Stepnell Photo Library (055) 62 6371
Northside Productions (03) 329 8710
Scoopix (03) 521 2233
Stock Photos (03) 699 7600
Stock Shots (03) 877 4455
Top Pix (03) 699 3868
Winter Light (03) 882 2461

PHOTO LIBRARIES: WESTERN AUSTRALIA
Jiri Lochman (09) 342 8821
Leon Bird Stock Shots (09) 444 7971
Max Head Photo Library (09) 305 1188
Photo Index (09) 481 0375
Phototone (09) 448 8455
Profile (09) 384 1980
Stock Glamour Library (09) 447 8663

DESIGNERS: NEW SOUTH WALES
A & L Barnum (02) 436 0363
Alex Thorby (043) 60 1993
Anderson Gosewinckel (02) 660 4163
Andi Cole Design (02) 922 4363
Andrew Lewis & Co. (02) 959 4800
Annette Harcus Design (02) 327 4013
Anthony Villani (02) 212 3144
Art Direction Associates (02) 923 1599
Barton Wendt (02) 360 4307
Belbin & Assoc (02) 922 1417
Billy Blue Group (02) 957 2844. Page 70
Blackall Design (02) 918 9460
Bluetree Design (02) 357 7966. Page 56
Bois de Chesne (02) 949 4035
Brass Tacks (02) 925 0822
Burley, Katon, Halliday (02) 332 2233
Carla Maitland (02) 484 7707
Cato Design Inc. (02) 327 3866
Christina Beaumont (02) 986 1106
Chris Wilson Design (02) 810 4673
Cliff Burk Design (02) 957 1223
Commercial Graphic Studio (02) 212 1800
Corke Art (02) 484 6320
Corlette Design (02) 439 4922. Page 58
Corporate Design Serv (02) 699 9111
Crackerjack Design Group (02) 332 2866. Page 52
Craig Sambrook Design (02) 955 6016
Creative Graphics (02) 699 2399
Creative Solutions (02) 437 4415
David Graphics (02) 698 9866
David Heweston (02) 331 1560
Designfield (02) 328 7366
Design Firm (02) 955 0232
Design Group (02) 957 1844
Design Resource (02) 906 1711
Design 17 (02) 439 6739
Design Sphere (02) 963 7733
Eymont Kin-Yee Design (02) 361 5322
Don Stephens Design (02) 868 2582
Gallaher & Assoc. (02) 957 1655
Ginns Design (02) 281 1366
Graphic Workshop (02) 969 8500
Hand Graphics (02) 439 4437
Hans Hulsbosch Design (02) 922 6188
Horniak & Canny (02) 290 2322. Page 82, 113
Ian Hammer (02) 955 4177
Ian Thwaites (02) 957 5361
Impact Graphics (02) 663 4987
Inhaus Productions (02) 631 7100. Page 130
Innovart (02) 953 4406
Intelink (02) 358 5333
Invetech Design (02) 319 2999
Isis Design (02) 261 3500
Jane Hord Graphic Design (02) 361 4284
Jeff Young (02) 958 5888
Jenssen Design (02) 922 7500
John Gittoes Graphic Design (02) 281 4273
John Morgan (02) 955 3257
Jon Hawley (02) 360 3100
Jones & Guihen (02) 968 1704
Kameruka Design (02) 958 7105. Page 131, 125
Kannegieter & Vogan Graphics (02) 436 0677
Katherine Wilkinson (02) 692 8782
Keith Theobald (02) 957 2322
Ken Andrews Design (02) 212 1800
Ken & Robin Clifton (02) 953 5110
Kennedy Goldsmith Graphics (02) 281 1481
KVB (02) 922 4278
Livingstone Clark (02) 957 2601. Page 72
Lorraine Hal Graphic Designer (02) 555 7492
McAlpine Design (02) 977 3821
Margo Snape Studio (02) 906 1106
Mark Denning (02) 439 2088
Mary Davy Design (02) 360 4422
Mike Ashby (02) 807 4082
Michael Farrell (02) 32 2538
Murray Van Design (02) 957 1615
Nelson Leong (02) 332 2933
Ngaire Waller (02) 411 3610
Nigel Louez (02) 922 5270
Oz Graphics (02) 963 7722
Passanisi & Assoc (02) 439 4744
Penny Davis Design (02) 32 2538
Professional Graphics (02) 818 4044
Propaganda/FHA (02) 929 8912
Quackers (02) 33 4042
Rap Art (02) 969 9800
Raymond Bennett Design (02) 959 5777
Recreation Studios (02) 929 5580
Reno Visual Communication (02) 698 4388
Richard Cornielje (02) 957 6388
Richardson Design (02) 552 4165. Page 68
Jennifer Richardson (02) 439 2694. Page 46
Rick Reynolds (02) 929 4849
Ritchie Thorburn Design (02) 692 0566. Page 80
Robyn Ellison Design (02) 438 5591
Ross Barr (02) 929 0055
Serov Design (02) 789 1801
Sharrin Rees Graphic Design (02) 360 3070
Spatchurst Design (02) 358 5866
Stewart Hamilton Design (02) 969 7428
Stig Ehnbom (02) 439 6844
Stone Davies (02) 439 8100
Sue Foster (02) 211 1396
Suzy King Design (02) 906 5634. Page 54
Tasos Polydorou (02) 281 4900
Ted Krzeminski Graphics (02) 457 8104
The Marketing Pack (02) 555 1505
The Packaging Lady (02) 958 5100
Tina Young (02) 552 2064
TKR Graphics (02) 633 2151
Tony Foster Graphic Design (02) 449 9073
Tony Ross Graphics (02) 436 1595
Underline (02) 436 1144
Viscomdesign Pty Ltd (02) 452 4431
Visual Banquet (02) 449 5859
Zlata Creative Design (02) 906 2468

DESIGNERS: SOUTH AUSTRALIA
Advertising Design Studio (08) 373 3858. Page 133
Andrew Rankine Design (08) 262 5220
Axis Graphix (08) 337 7024
Baxtergrafik (08) 271 6392
Brent Parks & Co. (08) 364 1402
Brenton Murray (08) 333 2224
Burton Nesbitt Graphic Design (08) 212 2968
Cairns Graphic Design (08) 332 5340
Cato Johnson (08) 333 2333
Charles Cannon (08) 232 3204. Page 137
Craig Costello (08) 258 1232
Design Energy (08) 223 6108
Designhaus (08) 232 1599
Designs in Graphic Art (08) 212 5180
Draper Honeywill Graphic Design (08) 373 4040
Ed Cooke (08) 362 3196
Grant Jorgensen Design (08) 271 7753
Hilditch Design Company (08) 363 0747
Ian Kidd Design (08) 332 0000. Page 106
Imaginaction Studios (08) 212 6175
John Nowland Design (08) 212 2037
John Vivian Art Design (08) 362 4423
Jolly Good Design (08) 239 0344
Julie Johinke Graphic Design (08) 79 5661
Leske and Co (08) 389 6742
Maurice Linehan Design (08) 278 8024
Pagoda Design (08) 352 6430
Promographics & Design (08) 294 5677
Simetri (08) 362 4888
Spyker Graphic Design Studio (08) 371 0650
Stephen Payne Design (08) 267 5471
The Peter Maxwell Company (08) 31 1199
Woods Bagot Graphics (08) 212 7600

DESIGNERS: VICTORIA

Ad Shop (03) 793 2737. Page 84
Adstract Art (03) 417 2163. Page 76
Alex Stitt & Partner (03) 240 8451. Page 45
Allegro Graphics (03) 836 1600
Amanda Roach Design (03) 521 1602
Anagram Design (03) 428 3695
Art House (03) 877 2744
Art Thieves (03) 654 1511
Anthony Trufitt (03) 846 1452
Art Attack (03) 699 4271
Artifishal (03) 417 7420
Asprey Di Donato (03) 388 0543. Page 90
Avenues Design (03) 650 3142. Page 121
B & B Design (03) 529 8999. Page 64
Barry Broadbent Design (03) 699 7820
Bauer Design (03) 654 8822
Beavis Design (03) 560 9744
Bevers Design (03) 819 5022. Page 78
Bigtime Design (03) 267 2202
Bill Caldwell (03) 699 8694
Brent Ward (03) 699 4179
Brian Pearce & Partners (03) 51 6998
Brian Sadgrove Design (03) 690 8977. Page 62
Bruce Duncan Design (03) 429 1411
By Design (03) 329 5499
Building On Design (03) 596 8051
Carola Easte (03) 428 8225. Page 74
Cartwright Design (03) 696 5050
Cato Design Inc (03) 429 6577
Chameleon Graphics (03) 598 5214
City Graphics (03) 600 0977. Page 111
Condon Payne Terry (03) 690 7803
Cosmos Julien (03) 534 2819
Cozzolino Ellett Design D'Vision (03) 882 9711
Cunningham & Cummings (03) 690 4477
Cutter Design & Illustration (03) 25 4268
Dan Fogel (03) 800 1413
Daryl Turner (03) 890 4509. Page 139
David Bryant (03) 525 6619
David Charland Graphics (054) 41 4372
David Hughes Design (03) 419 9288
David Lancashire Design (03) 427 1766
David Sampietro (03) 882 2616
Dennis Ogden (03) 885 8276
Design Synergy (03) 696 5577
Design Wise (03) 699 4696
Dezign (03) 481 7266
Dietman Innes (03) 654 5204
Elizabeth Wells Design (03) 690 9452
Emery Vincent Assoc (03) 699 3822. Page 115, 141
Emmerson Design (03) 752 1204
Flett Henderson and Arnold (03) 429 6888. Page 88
Fulvio Sussan Designs (03) 347 0705
Genevieve Rees Design (03) 529 5579
Gerry Graig Design (03) 690 2732
Gillian Vale (03) 555 1246
Glenn Ball Design (03) 807 8507
Grant Gittus Graphics (03) 690 6703
Graphic Ideas (03) 670 6338
Graphic-Ideation (03) 383 4171
Gray Graphics (03) 817 4505
Great Graphics (03) 266 1626
Grubb & Grubb (03) 646 2215
Gumboot Graphics (03) 754 8226
Harry Simon & Assoc (03) 529 2411
Helen Kent (03) 696 3400. Page 127
Henry Birman Design (018) 352 529
Honey Clark (03) 429 2084
Hutter Graphics (03) 696 2203
If Only (03) 696 5366
Impact Graphics (03) 650 2081
Inc Design (03) 690 7343
Ink n Essence (03) 51 4571
Integraphiq (03) 428 8225. Page 74
Jan Phillips Studio (03) 529 5906
Jas Art (03) 698 0299
Jim Finlayson (03) 531 4257
Kajetan Design Group (03) 521 1333
Karon Design (03) 794 0956
Len Trenkner (03) 329 9982
Lucas Seater Design (03) 417 1464
MH Graphics (03) 347 7758
Malcolm Thomson Design (03) 419 5802
Malpass and Burrows (03) 696 6422
Marjorie Boag Design (03) 267 4218
Mark Littler Design (03) 266 3895
Marshall Arts (03) 534 7721
Max Robinson & Assoc. (03) 51 3000. Page 60, 123, 105
Meg Robertson (03) 326 5901
Michele Moorehouse (03) 529 6859
Miller Design (03) 531 9444
Ned Culic Design (03) 534 6445
Nerve Centre (03) 690 5088
Newton and Rowan (052) 21 7557
Noel Pennington (03) 537 2977
Noni Edmunds (03) 528 4446
Nuttshell Graphics (03) 329 8988. Page 66
On The Ball (03) 326 6666. Page 86
Optimum Design (03) 646 5033
Optus Graphics (03) 690 7548
Origination (03) 482 2500
Partners In Design (03) 690 8593
Peter Campbell (03) 510 2668. Page 144
Peter Hocking (03) 380 2621
Prismagraphics Pty Ltd (03) 240 8033
Rankin Design Group (03) 862 2299. Page 143
Returb (03) 429 4147
Robert Rosetzky Design (03) 614 2958. Page 40
Roger Simpson (03) 696 5577
Ros Lawson Design (03) 690 3428
Rosie Harris-Grubb (03) 534 7755
Ross Koenig (03) 829 1766
Russell Bevers Design (03) 819 5022. Page 78
Russell Jackson Graphics (03) 690 6344
Spencer Davies (03) 233 2481
SR Graphics Design (03) 690 2255
Stephan Bowhacz Design (03) 529 6944
Steve Blenheim Design (03) 529 5658
Steve Chapman Design (03) 848 3193
Steve Osborne Graphic Design (03) 329 2370
Storey and Design (03) 329 5770
Struck and Spink (03) 592 1424
Stuart Pettigrew Design (03) 529 1037
T.G. Design (03) 427 9993
The Bakery Design Studio (03) 51 9412
The Design Dept (03) 690 5744
Thunderbird Graphics (03) 696 6600
Toby Purves (03) 699 9191
Towns & Co. (03) 654 2544
Trigrafix (03) 427 0899
Turner (03) 696 6994
Ultimate Images Design (03) 583 0553
Visual Identity (03) 690 7812
Warwick Cruise Graphic Design (03) 509 9457. Page 128
Wellington House (03) 529 6944. Page 44.
World of Wonders (03) 417 6863

ILLUSTRATORS & DESIGNERS: NORTHERN TERRITORY

Alternative Studio B (089) 81 9585
Teresa Chang (089) 27 4748
Desert Graphics (089) 52 4399
Drawing Room (089) 81 5918
Focal Design (089) 52 3053
Yolanda Illana (089) 41 0291
Imprint Design (089) 27 2457
R & K Kessing (089) 52 4399
Presentations (089) 81 3646
Territory Editorial (089) 81 9341
Ardys Zoellner (089) 81 8530

ILLUSTRATORS & DESIGNERS: QUEENSLAND

AALL Graphics (07) 341 3720
Architectural Art (07) 393 1698
Art Attack (071) 42 1306
Max Bannah (07) 371 4956
Paul Barnes (07) 355 7608
Jeff Blundell (071) 45 3062
Jill Brose (07) 369 8367
Fred Bruinsma (07) 288 1370
Buzz Creative (07) 832 0146
Paul Byrne (07) 369 1211
Mike Champ (07) 204 6356
Martin De Lang (07) 375 1960
Concept Communications (07) 252 8322
Michael De Nada (07) 844 8787
Matt Epple (07) 844 8787
Ziya Eris (07) 368 3249
Philip Flower (07) 848 3573
Fryer Designs (07) 366 3344
John Garnsworthy (07) 221 6465
Grunwald Design (075) 34 2468
John Harrison (07) 832 3123
Brent Harvey (07) 844 8787
Christine Hayes (07) 832 2529
Hush Creative Design (07) 832 5729
Martin Johncock (07) 202 7575
Kert Artstaff Creative (07) 368 3682
Roslyn Klauke (07) 399 8751
Stephen Lee (07) 832 6170
Peter Letts (07) 34 6975
Zelman Lew (075) 55 1599
Patrice Louttit (07) 376 4974
Jennifer Marchant (07) 854 1998
Simon McLean (07) 358 5525
Minale Tattersfield Bryce (07) 831 4149
Carolyn Morgan Design (07) 221 2184
Stuart Powell (07) 393 1688
David Randall (07) 265 3247
Gregory Rogers (07) 399 4895
Trevor Ruth (077) 71 3549
Sue Schmidt (07) 832 3123
Cliff Sheldrake (07) 852 1807
Glen Singleton (07) 829 4427
Belinda Stewart (02) 844 8787
Hugh Stewart-Kilklick (07) 369 2315
Ann Stirling (07) 378 1808
Michael Stuart (07) 844 8787
Louise Thomas (07) 252 4709
Bill Thurgood (07) 846 1307
Barrie Tucker (075) 91 2645
Dennis Veal (07) 358 1233
West Side Studio (07) 844 8787

ILLUSTRATORS & DESIGNERS: TASMANIA

Advertising Art (002) 31 0022
Bush Telegraph Design (003) 34 1212
Robert Clegg (002) 44 4037
Creative Concepts (002) 23 2556
Creative Studio (003) 32 0344
Creative Studio (002) 21 1242
Dazeley Studio (002) 21 1210
Garfield Design (002) 34 2177
Dennis Green (002) 23 6726
Graphic Plus (002) 66 4405
Gary Kennedy Graphics (002) 23 39[illegible]8
Jane James (002) 31 1530
Roger Murphy & Assoc. (002) 29 6147
Paperworks (002) 27 9112
Press Art (002) 30 0675
Pro Art (002) 23 2458
Graham Ristow (002) 66 4405
W. Strickland (004) 25 1577
Stutter & Assoc (002) 28 3879
Taswegia (004) 24 8300
Rod Taylor Graphics (004) 24 2279
Vision Design (002) 23 4733

ILLUSTRATORS & DESIGNERS WESTERN AUSTRALIA

Fred Alberts (09) 382 4619
Art & Design (09) 322 6459
Art Innovations (09) 382 1782
Artworks (09) 364 8992
Don Baker Illustrations (09) 481 0573
Bassett-Scarfe Graphics (09) 321 7585
Martin Beseler Airbrush (09) 341 4755
Steve Bevan (09) 321 5133
Danny Breen (09) 382 4860
Chameleon Designs (07) 227 9733. Page 117
Brian Danton (09) 384 3081
Corporate Design Centre (09) 388 2844
John Davies Designer (09) 368 2477
Peter Dickson (09) 470 1262
Dillon Graphics (09) 481 6146
Philip Evans (09) 381 2277
Robert Gregory (09) 387 8026
Haddock Graphics (09) 367 6930
Geoff Haines Design (09) 291 9307
Meredith Hardy (09) 227 9806
Rose Hart (09) 453 1413
Karin Hearn (09) 328 6306
John Hulme (09) 470 1262
Vernon Jones (09) 382 1417
Longley Jones Graphics (09) 322 6762
Rick Lambert (09) 367 3644
Jo Laney Design (09) 388 2077
Langoulant Graphics (09) 341 5559
Leeves Design (09) 227 9226
Linear Graphics (09) 382 4941
Marshall Illustrations (09) 401 6881
Adrian Oats (09) 276 9067
Peachy Productions (09) 381 7536
Chris Spaven (09) 322 5957
Russell Springham (09) 470 1262
Sumner Graphics (09) 387 5833
Brett Stevens (09) 382 2903
Sheryl Stevens (09) 381 6894
Technical Illustrations (09) 321 7292
Technology Arts (09) 321 7292
Turner Graphics (07) 321 3811. Page 109
James Weinbren (09) 383 3798

ILLUSTRATORS: NEW SOUTH WALES

Tony Ablen (02) 957 5553
Kerri Ainsworth (02) 588 3134
Louis Alach (02) 922 6811
Ambler & Haycraft (02) 489 5902
Ken Andrews (02) 212 1800
Jay Antablian (02) 212 6815
Robin Appleby (02) 941 298
Alan Arkinstall (02) 958 3485
Artworks (02) 439 4399
Graham Austin (02) 909 1988
Graham Back (02) 906 1262
Mitchell Barnes (02) 332 4654
Wendy Bastock (02) 774 3667
Bazza Art (02) 411 1077
Russell Bean (02) 923 1600
Josef Beniac (02) 438 2899
O. Bilauczak (02) 923 1283
Jennifer Black (02) 957 3066
Ted Blackall (02) 955 6032. Page 135
Bev & Gerry Blake (02) 331 1210
Blue Feather (02) 810 4044
Blue Tree (02) 909 2656
Peter Bollinger (02) 555 1166
Brass Tacks (02) 925 0022
Gregory Bridges (02) 631 7100
Nigel Buchanan (02) 211 1396
Gordon Bye (02) 981 4211
Peter Calvitto (02) 427 3539
Philip Campbell (042) 27 3213
Barry Campbell (02) 959 5713
Vaughan Campbell (02) 938 5249
Bruce Carlisle (02) 451 5737
David Carroll (02) 922 3836
Keith Chatto (02) 587 5586
Teena Clerke (02) 357 7488
Clop (02) 92 7707
Robert Coady (02) 929 7180
Philip Cornell (02) 955 4955
Paul Cottrell (02) 357 7488
John Coye (02) 922 3836
Donna Cross NZ 4-862 727
Simon Darby (02) 957 3106
Eric David (02) 957 2047
Mark Davidson (02) 439 4922
Wendy de Paauw (02) 923 1717
Dial-a-Cartoon (02) 969 7455
Beth Dockar (02) 909 3143
Ken Done (02) 698 8555
Mario Donk (043) 90 8843
Barry Donohoo (02) 929 9837
Drawing Book Studios (02) 922 6811
Leonie Dubois (02) 908 2962
Earl St Artists (02) 398 6652
Phillip Enfield (02) 365 0389
Christer Ericksson (02) 451 5706
European Grey (02) 660 6926
Every Picture (02) 357 7088
Alan Ewart (02) 331 2310
Peter Fairlie (02) 959 3133
Manfred Farrell (02) 810 3674
Michael Farrell (02) 32 2538
Suzanne Faye (02) 660 4282
Simon Fenton (02) 521 2132
Arthur Filloy (02) 929 7145
Sue Foster (02) 211 1396
Lloyd Foye (02) 959 3133

Darrell Fraser (02) 929
Frog Hollow (02) 968 1090
Ethna Gallacher (02) 957 1571
Ron Galliman (02) 692 8952
Greg Gillespie (02) 971 2211
John Gittoes (02) 281 4273
Mike Golding (02) 211 2243
Kim Graham (02) 929 7180
Stephen Graham (02) 953 0580
Graphic Harmony (02) 929 5800
Beryl Green (02) 267 6073
Patrice Guilbert (02) 489 1641
Helen Halliday (02) 960 4920
Bonita Halm (02) 398 2579
George Hamori (02) 327 6667
Peter Hanbury (066) 28 3936
Craig Handley (02) 922 6811
Jim Hansen (02) 332 4467
Bruce Harkness (02) 909 3143
Danielle Hatherley (02) 92 6032
Chris Hauge (02) 560 6280
Jon Hawley (02) 360 3100
John Haycraft (02) 428 5902
Berndt Heinrich (02) 918 0832
Glen Hewett (066) 24 3651
David Holler (02) 955 7147
Phillip Holiday (02) 955 7147
Jo Anne Hook (02) 922 6811
Hooroo Studio (02) 411 3637
Michael Howard (02) 909 1223
Brian Howes (062) 85 1191
Richard Hughes (02) 922 6811
Roz Hyndman (02) 282 0740
Ikuko (02) 922 3297
Inhaus Productions (02) 631 7100
Grant Johnson (02) 909 3143
Janet Jones (02) 698 3127
Ulf Kaiser (02) 817 4373
Frants Kantor (02) 331 2284
Helena Karnolz (02) 929 6173
Reg Kassell (02) 644 2620
Keith Kelly (02) 467 1094
Scott Kennedy NZ 4 862 727
Myriam Kin-Yee (02) 361 5322
David M King (02) 922 6172
David Kirshner (02) 969 9129
Frank Knight (062) 81 1289
Sebastian Lakosta (02) 918 6873
Alexander Lavroff (02) 909 3143
Alan Lawrence (02) 959 3133
Phillip Layzell (02) 360 2999
Kerrie Leishman (02) 690 1259
Joe Leong (02) 957 6209
Simon Letch (02) 360 3487
Peter Leuver (02) 44 6117
Philip Little (02) 929 6013
Michael Lodge (02) 30 8512
Frank Lopez (02) 922 6811
Steve Lyons (02) 922 6811
Ron Lyons (047) 39 3664
Bruce Madden (02) 925 0404
Ed Marr (02) 81 1075
Greg McAlpine (02) 977 3821
Brendan McCarthy (02) 357 7488
Meg McDonald (02) 476 5050
Scott McDougall (02) 959 3133
Steve McHugh (02) 955 6016

Iain McKellar (02) 439 4793
Murray MacKenzie (066) 55 1743
Bruce Madden (02) 925 0404
Felicity Meyer (02) 51 2734
Mike & Marie (02) 959 3133
John Mitchell (02) 357 4209
Julie Morris (02) 437 6811
Miguel Munoz (02) 929 7180
Peter Murphy (02) 831 1962
Olev Muska (02) 519 5970
David Naseby (02) 953 7883
Kevin O'Donnell (02) 929 2344
Barry Olive (02) 957 5598
Otto & Chris (043) 79 1266
Judith Palmisano (02) 90 2270
Gwyn Perkins (02) 99 3783
Bradley Pike (02) 30 8765
Theo Politis (062) 57 6947
Marilyn Pride (02) 560 5648
Belinda Pring (02) 922 2320
Proudfoot & Khoo (02) 360 5226
Alan Puckett (02) 817 3605
Tony Pyrzakowski (02) 438 3669
Duffy Regan (02) 798 4530
Graham Rendoth (02) 698 4388
John Richards (02) 451 1765
Gordon Rigby-Smith (02) 44 5692
Ken Rinkel (02) 959 3133
Philip Ritchie (02) 692 0708
Skye Rogers (02) 810 4154
Yoli Salmona (02) 398 9857
Kim Sandel (02) 909 3095
Roland Schicht (02) 371 6419
Maurice Schlesinger (02) 399 6650
Robyn Schofield (02) 922 3313
John Scott (02) 484 6939
John Scott (02) 939 6237
Scribbles Art (02) 929 2500
Peter Shannon (02) 957 3553
David Shapter (02) 969 1351
Lendon Shaw (02) 451 6903
Jeannie Sher (02) 959 3133
Louis Silvestro (02) 955 4592
Margo Snape (02) 906 1106
Greg Somers (02) 438 2114
Paul Stanish (02) 957 1844
Ron Stannard (02) 451 2404
Noel Stapleton (02) 634 2832
Don Stephens (02) 868 2582
Alan Stomann (02) 929 2522
Guiletta Stomann (02) 955 7711
Shirley Sykes (02) 476 4633
Gail Sylvester (02) 387 3511
Derryn Tal (02) 327 3540
Bernard Tate (02) 439 1003
Gerad Taylor (02) 922 5818
Alex Thorby (043) 60 1993
Mark Tremlett (02) 958 7094
Hideo Tsubono (02) 953 9523
Stephen Vanderhorst (02) 588 7778
Katrina Van Gendt (02) 929 2522
Joop Van Heusden (02) 960 4950
Spike Wademan (02) 929 7180
David Wardman (02) 331 2748
Ross Waters (02) 451 4219
David Welch (02) 953 8828
Bob West (02) 929 2344

John Westblade (02) 922 3836
Bruce Whatley (02) 922 4098
Mick White (02) 920 5918
Peter White (02) 908 2620
Liam White (02) 923 1717
Stephen White (02) 597 3394
Geoff Williams (066) 842 2923
Chris Wilson (02) 810 4673
Diedre Wilson (02) 909 3095
Faye Wilson (047) 82 4663
Rodney Wong (02) 412 1013
Dave Wood (02) 922 2320
Melanie Wood (02) 909 3095
Morna Wood (02) 922 6811
Mike Worrall (02) 959 3133
John Yates (02) 331 1389
Tony Yuletich (02) 922 1005
Serge Zaleski (02) 439 6636
Alvaro Zarelli (02) 909 3143

ILLUSTRATORS: SOUTH AUSTRALIA

Graham Abraham (08) 281 1909
George Aldridge (085) 22 1972
Kerry Argent (08) 42 3771
Arty Stuff (08) 274 6096
Don Berry (08) 364 2166
Bright Tiger (08) 231 6707
Peter Broelman (08) 252 1818
Simon Clarke (08) 252 1818
Ian Crilly (08) 42 2054
Sandra Elms (08) 223 4060
Peter Goeldi (08) 79 7126
Vivienne Goodman (08) 363 2333
Amanda Graham (08) 267 1022
Doreen Gristwood (08) 272 9560
Donna Gynell (08) 271 7753
Karen Hahn (08) 45 5925
Rita Hall (08) 339 2321
Scott Hartshorne (08) 332 5822
Sally Heinrich (08) 272 5161
Karl Josef Horvat (08) 263 4454
Andrew Humphries (08) 224 0136
Bronia Ivanbrook (08) 42 5017
David Kennett (08) 79 4147
Graham McArthur (08) 223 2086
Stuart McLauchlan (08) 223 4060
Carol McLean-Carr (08) 269 6753
Robert Marshall (08) 332 0268
Brenton Murray (08) 333 2224
Daniel New (085) 22 3603
Sue O'Loughlin (08) 332 0628
Maria Parrott (08) 223 4060
Roger Roberts (08) 232 2622
Tim Sanders (08) 278 8484
David Schaefer (08) 295 4995
Leslie Scholes (085) 22 4976
Terry Sciascia (08) 267 1022
Simetri (08) 42 3762
Peter Smeets (08) 332 7382
Craig Smith (08) 42 2315
Maere Smith (08) 42 2315
Peter Smith (08) 332 2289
Kevin Stead (08) 223 4121
Craig Stevens (08) 252 1041
Debbie Strauss (08) 223 4060
Tellygraph (08) 239 0609
William Tennant (08) 223 4060

Lincoln Tiver (08) 272 8855
Jim Tsinganos (08) 223 4060
Robert A. Walter (08) 333 2840
Wilson Graphics (08) 227 0132
Lisa Young (08) 223 7662

ILLUSTRATORS: VICTORIA
Acme Graphics (03) 51 4295
Admaker (03) 699 3035
Drew Aitken (03) 458 4831
Alexander Andre (03) 842 5957
Joy Antoine (03) 529 2326
Peter Arnold (03) 482 2766
Art Associates (03) 266 8618
Art Direction (03) 699 9007
Art House (The) (03) 877 2453
Con Aslanis (03) 521 1080
David Baker (03) 534 7030
Louise Baker (03) 240 9019
Lorrie Banks (03) 521 1386
Peter Barclay (03) 696 3622
Amanda Barratt (03) 562 1938
Patricia Barth (03) 699 9548
Robyn Becker (03) 557 5501
Paolo Bellini (03) 531 9226
Gordon Bird (03) 696 3202
Don Black (03) 596 3380
Ray Black (03) 696 5366
Jerzy Boberski (03) 861 8595
Colin Bodie (03) 527 5483
Fred Briggs (03) 699 5574
Keith Brown (03) 690 9952
Julian Bruere (03) 489 5713
Denis Bryans (03) 819 3675
David Bryant (03) 525 6619
Derek Butler (03) 663 7469
Liga Byron (03) 266 1550
Mark Cairns (052) 29 4982
Daryl Carnahan (03) 51 8841
Bruce Cavalier (03) 531 7453
Anthony Chiappin (03) 592 2139
Brian Clinton (03) 560 4351
Ray Condon (03) 690 7316
Tony Constantino (03) 531 2114
Geoff Cook (03) 509 3919
Robin Cowcher (03) 534 8005
Ned Culic (03) 534 6445
Neil Curtis (03) 531 4468
Priscilla Cutter (03) 885 4268
Bob Davidson (03) 266 1550
Jeffrey Diamond (03) 525 1524
John Dickens (03) 484 7853
Klara Donath (03) 459 0665
Adrian Dyson (03) 525 4666
Peter Edgeley (03) 699 1756
Levent Efe (03) 646 5945
Richard Evans (03) 699 3035
Edgar Gambin (03) 785 1439
Dianne Gameson (03) 699 1571
Kerri Gibbs (03) 537 2352
Will Goodwin (03) 696 6902
Graphic Connection (03) 482 2766
John Grbic (03) 684 6568
Betty Greenhatch (03) 696 3336
Simon Greenwood (03) 267 6750
Matt Grogan (03) 527 8021
George Haddon (03) 696 3212
Geoff Hayes (03) 592 9146
Chris Henley (03) 481 0811
David Higgins (054) 75 2419
Guy Holt (03) 347 9824
Vanessa Hughes (03) 531 2445
Paul Ingoldby (03) 51 4571
Instant Images (03) 529 7775
Ali Jabbar (03) 652 2157
Cosmos Julien (03) 534 2819
Patrick Kan (03) 489 9139
Geoff Kelly (03) 882 9780
Graham Kelly (03) 525 6620
Ron Kirk (03) 347 6840
John Kirkland (03) 754 3106
Cam Knuckey (03) 529 7401
Elspeth Lacey (03) 527 7117
Scott Lacey (03) 882 6232
Bruce Lauchlan (03) 690 1947
John Lazzano (03) 690 7343
Connell Lee (053) 41 4588
Ulrich Lehmann (03) 584 4441
Tony Lester (03) 571 0991
Joe Levine (03) 269 2777
Chris Lynch (03) 859 1580
Robert Mancini (03) 397 7671
Rod Marsh (03) 264 1133
Phil Masters (03) 699 5574
Jan Matuszczak (03) 844 2090
Ian McCausland (03) 525 3766
Keith McEwen (03) 844 2306
Craig McGill (03) 527 5234
Roy McLoed (03) 690 4075
Kikitsa Michalantos (03) 489 2503
David Miller (03) 722 1486
J. Mor (03) 428 1689
Peter Morris (03) 894 2563
Patricia Mullins (03) 417 3289
Shane Nagle (03) 882 7860
David Nelson (03) 534 5424
Nerve Centre (03) 690 5088
Dianne Nethercott (03) 509 8419
Jack Newnham (03) 690 4663
Stephan Nieckrash (03) 569 9140
Betina Ogden (03) 866 1021
Chris Orr (03) 482 2766
Mike Osborne (03) 867 7917
Deborah Page (03) 580 4923
Lillian Pagonis (03) 525 6619
Kevin Parker (03) 437 1943
Chris Payne (03) 690 5531
Mark Payne (03) 718 2866
Craig Penny (03) 525 6619
Chris Petrie (03) 578 8476
Bartek Pisz (03) 380 4251
Jenny Phillips (054) 22 1496
Doug Pitt (03) 482 2766
Fay Plamka (03) 537 2352
Margaret Power (03) 527 4330
Darren Price (03) 534 6204
Jon Quinn (053) 45 6378
Annie Quinn (03) 521 1154
Sanno Raymond (03) 429 4247
Genevieve Rees (03) 529 5579
Kim Roberts-Smith (03) 882 6206
Colin Robson (03) 699 8404
Geoff Rogers (03) 699 3056
Alan Salisbury (03) 51 7161
Deborah Savin (03) 578 9869
Cornelia Selover (03) 537 1905
Barnaby Shephard (03) 435 2803
Bob Shields (03) 597 0464
Cameron Singleton (03) 818 5229
Mark Smith (03) 350 5686
Peter Smith (03) 885 5235
Mark Sofilas (03) 267 3671
Walter Stacjer (03) 527 5699
Chantal Stewart (03) 528 1494
Alexander Stitt (03) 240 8451
Heather Strahan (03) 500 9619
Peter Syle (03) 529 6642
Richard Szymczuk (03) 500 9024
Gary Taylor (054) 33 2547
Clyde Terry (03) 690 5615
Norm Tilley (03) 690 4008
Marg Towt (03) 482 2766
Mitch Vane (03) 525 4483
Annie Vanston (03) 521 1020
Gaston Vanzet (03) 439 8306
Peter Viska (03) 521 1050
Vizkidz (03) 266 1550
Jane Wallace-Smith (03) 690 3633
Brent Ward (03) 699 4179
Raymond Webbe (03) 583 0958
Wegtoons (03) 729 5609
Julian Whittaker (053) 681 366
Kerri Winnen (03) 699 1769
Michael Wilkin (03) 696 5370
Sarah Wilkins (03) 882 0024
Ross Willsmore (03) 690 4641
Bill Wood (03) 862 3269
Diane Worland (03) 534 2440
Anita Xhafer (03) 690 3035
Jacqui Young (03) 537 1337

TV COMMERCIAL PRODUCTION: NEW SOUTH WALES

A Couple A Cowboys (02) 953 8155
A1 Blockbuster Film (02) 527 4444
Amidell (02) 261 5488
Andrew Vial Film Production (02) 922 3297
Aust Capital TV (062) 41 1000
Axolotl (02) 331 6335
B.C. Communicators (02) 958 2100
Berry's Creative (02) 909 1211
Bill McCrow (02) 958 1922
Blackthorn Productions (02) 807 4371
Brian McDuffie Productions (02) 436 3144
Camfilm Production Services (02) 417 7777
Canberra Media Productions (062) 58 2846
Challenges Accepted (02) 328 6133
Chateau Productions (02) 699 9658
Cinepix Films (02) 99 4729
Commercial Picture Makers (02) 818 5055
Communication Partners (062) 48 9622
Corporate Productions (02) 958 2100
Crown Communications (02) 906 3020
Cynthia Palmer Prod (02) 438 2751
David Douglas Productions (02) 969 8177
David Flatman Prod (02) 949 5199
Designads of Australia (02) 922 4200
Desmond & Bray (02) 957 1599
Electric Shadow (02) 419 6759
Enigma Productions (02) 438 3195
Essential Film Productions (02) 327 3077
Eureka Film Productions (02) 959 3388
EVS Group (02) 406 5622
Facelift Productions (02) 331 7097
Film Business and Partners (02) 281 8380
Film De Luxford (02) 356 3066
Film Graphics (02) 439 4233. Page 240
Film Trailers (02) 907 9383
Fontana Films (02) 906 2188
Gadonya Productions (02) 909 3070
Gracy Jones (02) 389 8225
Ibbetson & Cherry Film Co (02) 552 1288
Illustrated Radio (02) 969 7321
Image East (02) 957 2211
Iveson Clark Productions (02) 958 1244
Jaffa Picture Co (02) 954 0036
Jap-Art Productions (02) 908 1131
Jengrove (02) 913 1084
John Ashenhurst Films (02) 918 8324
Joyride Prod (02) 955 7923
J.S.A. Productions (02) 660 5357
Kookaburra Productions (02) 438 4344
Laramy Productions (02) 664 2259
Laughing Kookaburra (02) 331 3813
Lenswork Productions (02) 975 1338
Lighthouse Productions (02) 358 4422
Little Film Co (02) 411 1699
Look Film Productions (02) 436 1647
Mark Gould (02) 365 3306
MGP – McLennan Gilbert (02) 438 1797
Mantis Wildlife (02) 651 2323
Mason & Mason (02) 959 3500
Meaningful Eye Contact (02) 519 5854
Monster With 2 Toes (02) 358 1866
Mulcahy Enterprises (02) 953 1335
Motion Picture Assoc (043) 21 1211
National Recording Studios (062) 51 6333
Newark Productions (02) 958 4984
Omnitel (02) 439 6900
Paddington Film (02) 923 2377
Panorama Produtions (02) 212 1455
Perspective Sound & Vision (02) 969 4808
Peter Forrest-Smith (02) 427 4444
Pilgrim International (02) 906 1444
Pocknall Productions (068) 84 2178
Production Group (02) 406 0833
Pro Image (02) 439 5044
Quantum Leap (02) 906 3844
RK Productions (02) 810 1912
Red Ink (02) 437 5544
Reel Barrie Smith (02) 982 6927
Ron Windon (02) 960 0411
Rosebud (02) 436 0637
Ross Nichols (02) 439 7888
Ross Wood Productions (02) 331 5154
Seeka Productions (02) 957 5717
Shooting Gallery (02) 319 2822
Shot Productions (02) 550 1900
Silver Lining Productions (02) 267 2952
Sonic Vision (02) 281 2444
Sprowles Robertson Productions (02) 692 9755
Strauss Productions (02) 680 1595
Sydney Film (02) 922 5533
TVC Productions (02) 438 0578
Talking Picture Co (02) 437 5555
Telprom Pty Ltd (02) 887 9522
Terry Bunton Films (02) 281 3000
The Film Business (02) 281 8380.
The Sherwood Film Co (02) 360 3844
Thirty Seconds (02) 923 2088
220 Productions (02) 356 4201
Ulladulla Picture Co (02) 969 7599
Video Paint Brush Co (02) 888 9977
Video Team (02) 560 8307
Videopak (02) 451 8111
Visualeyes (02) 357 1444
Walker Clancy (02) 32 1112
Waterloo (02) 699 8755
West Botswana Productions (02) 816 3999
West St (02) 923 2291
Window Productions (02) 281 5333
XYZAP (02) 439 6691
Zoobs (02) 918 6637

TV COMMERCIAL PRODUCTION: QUEENSLAND

Abacus Pictures Pty (07) 878 1133
Boss Productions (07) 386 2965
Brisbane Media Centre (07) 252 5477
Concept TV Productions (075) 46 6700
Darling Downs TV (076) 32 2288
Dick Marks (07) 368 2722
East Coast Prod (075) 92 0077
En Cue Productions (07) 366 1107
Halliday Productions (07) 264 2475
Hoyts-Jumbuck Productions (07) 252 8577
Lucky Luciano Productions (07) 378 7681
Marlo Film & Video (077) 75 5011
Martin Williams Films (07) 371 0255
Media Dynamics Pty Ltd (07) 252 1273
Picture Place (075) 91 6655
Power House Productions (07) 846 2644
Roly Poly Pictures (07) 369 0444
Rupert & Bernstein (075) 91 6655
Starlite Film Prod (071) 96 8207
The Production Group (07) 846 2106
Up Stage Productions (07) 358 5511
Video Image Productions (07) 262 2400
Videoman Productions (07) 252 2697
Walt Deas Productions (075) 38 8231
Warneroo (07) 369 5925
Zenac Productions (07) 846 1388

TV COMMERCIAL PRODUCTION: SOUTH AUSTRALIA

Action Video (08) 42 5577
Channel 8 (08) 352 1115
Creative Video Productions (08) 231 9033
Dean Davis Productions (08) 231 3950
Directors Film & Video (08) 267 5911
EPCV (08) 31 3976
Ellson Productions (08) 362 8341
Film House (08) 239 0588
Giovanni Lovisetto (08) 339 6592
Great Southern Films (08) 223 4445
Headquarters (08) 232 1298
Milton Ingerson (08) 338 1666
N.S.W. Channel 9 (08) 267 0111
Newfilms (03) 340 0900
Pepper Studios (08) 363 0711
Pro-Image (08) 362 9971
Ray Beale (08) 42 5577
Roy Wooding (08) 31 0540
See It. Believe It. (08) 364 0868
Seethrufilm (08) 298 8562
Triad Productions (08) 79 3661
Viz-Ad (08) 269 5522
West Street (08) 923 2291
W.E.S. Productions (08) 223 1532
William Thomas Video (08) 294 4468

TV COMMERCIAL PRODUCTION: WESTERN AUSTRALIA

Barron Films Pty Ltd (09) 321 5924
Bush Christmas (09) 321 5924
CM Films (09) 328 8977
Compact Video (09) 382 1299
Comprod Channel 9 (09) 349 9999
Editel (09) 388 1544
Elephant (09) 388 1788
Ensemble (09) 481 8282.
Film Centre (09) 279 4544
Filmmakers (09) 293 4939
Filmwest (09) 271 7542
Geoff Oliver (09) 328 9877
Hugh Kitson Productions (09) 322 5453
Insignia (09) 388 1709
John Izzard (09) 481 6020
Kingwest Productions (09) 271 5348
Motion Picture Producers (09) 321 4137
On Line Video (09) 324 1600
Parmelia Productions (09) 384 8188
Pedro Video Productions (09) 480 9745
Peter Wynne and Assoc. (09) 309 1312
Picture Palace (09) 388 2323
Rembrand Films (09) 339 5348
Richard Oxenburgh Productions (09) 328 9488
Shots (09) 481 0103
Swan Commercial Productions (09) 349 9999
Total Production Group (09) 368 2399
Visual Image Productions (09) 328 3544
Western Images (09) 328 1977

TV COMMERCIAL PRODUCTION: VICTORIA
AAV (03) 699 1844
Acorn Film Productions (03) 429 4531
Aranda Film Productions (03) 596 4847
Australian Business Theatre (03) 241 6511
B & C Film Melbourne (03) 51 9806
Beat Films (03) 419 5838
Beaumaris Film Productions (03) 387 3686
Bendigo Street Productions (03) 420 3377
BOP (03) 696 4003
Cinematic Productions (03) 529 7496
Cohorts (03) 690 7711
David Campbell Productions (03) 690 7711
De Montigie and Assoc. (03) 509 1711
Digital Imaging (03) 690 8857
Essential Film Production (03) 240 0456
FM-TV Productions (03) 428 2967
Film Business and Partners (03) 690 5488
FilmHouse (03) 699 9722
Filmpartnership (03) 537 2655
Fortune Films (03) 696 4599
Gable Summertime (03) 534 0255
Gauche Productions (03) 534 1018
Great Southern Films (03) 267 6811
Greg Taylor Productions (03) 534 8051
HSV7 (03) 699 7777
Hips Film Productions (03) 690 6506
Horizon Films (03) 534 9443
Iloura (03) 645 3233
Janina Craig Services (03) 690 1229
Jay Film Productions (03) 690 6477
John Smallman Productions (03) 690 2233
Kingcroft (03) 563 9122
Leave it to Beaver (03) 690 4522
L. J. Productions (03) 419 5744
Lemac Film Video (03) 429 8588
Mighty Good Movies (03) 690 7711
Macrae and Way Productions (03) 690 1944
Miracle Picture Co (03) 696 1433
Moving Picture Company (03) 429 8444
Murray Collins Productions (03) 699 1404
Paul Drane (03) 690 6877
Pearly White Productions (03) 592 4656
Peter Coulter Productions (03) 534 8292
Peter Faiman (03) 826 2699
Photo Mation (03) 699 8799
Picnick (03) 326 5081
Pro Image (03) 614 4111
RKO Productions (03) 266 2253
Robert Imhoff Productions (03) 529 2144
Rod Kinnear (03) 707 3533
Ross Nicholls Productions (03) 699 4800
Roxy Productions (03) 690 9822
Short Stories (03) 646 2002
Sonicvision Productions (03) 690 4822
Super Vision Productions (03) 699 2666
Sykes and Dale (03) 699 4800
Taboo Productions (03) 211 1140
The Cottage (03) 232 4133
The Film Business and Partners (03) 690 5488
VTC (03) 534 8021
Video Paint Brush Co (03) 690 7499
Vitascope (03) 534 9211

FREELANCE AGENCIES: NEW SOUTH WALES
Available Now (02) 953 3323.
Camerons Management (02) 356 2155
Melanie Dames (02) 337 1488
Drawing Book (02) 922 6811
Every Picture Tells A Story (02) 357 7088
Film Techs (02) 971 1666
Alex Lavroff (02) 909 3143
Myriam's Artists (02) 699 8099
Merilake (02) 959 3133
The Names Agency (02) 550 5141
Stills (02) 356 2155
Tabs (02) 427 4444
Talkies (02) 498 3088
Top Technicians (02) 981 1622
TV Personnel (02) 411 8959

FREELANCE AGENCIES: QUEENSLAND
Queensland Film Crew (07) 391 4688
New Breed Stunts (07) 399 3177

FREELANCE AGENCIES: SOUTH AUSTRALIA
Crew Call (08) 332 2940
The Photographers Agent (08) 269 2825

FREELANCE AGENCIES: VICTORIA
Barbara Grange Management (03) 419 7133
Dux F M (03) 690 5527
Folio Representation (03) 525 4684
Freelancers Promotions (03) 598 5104
New Generation Stunts (03) 699 5233
Picture People (03) 391 9438
Wellington House (03) 529 6944

FREELANCE AGENCIES: WESTERN AUSTRALIA
Extra Extras (09) 481 7687
Tabs (09) 481 7687
Tabs FMP (09) 242 2311
W.A. Filmworkers (09) 335 9436
W.A. Freelancers (09) 444 3727

PRINT PRODUCTION CONSULTANTS: NEW SOUTH WALES.
Azzopardi, Nick (02) 412 4812
Belbin & Assoc (02) 953 8799
Carmen, David (02) 925 0022
Communicado (02) 51 5508
Dalton Begley (02) 957 5507
Design Group (02) 957 1844
Fahey Communications (02) 929 5011
Russell, Glen (02) 957 1286
Tumbarumba Productions (02) 552 1900
Weaver Productions (02) 555 7866
Youdale, Graham (02) 411 7455

PRINT PRODUCTION CONSULTANTS: QUEENSLAND.
Print Management Services (07) 252 9522
Printer Wholesalers (07) 359 8516
Print Link (07) 252 3432

PRINT PRODUCTION CONSULTANTS: VICTORIA.
Integration/Roger Neil (03) 510 2232
Kevin Fisher Pty Ltd (03) 895 0561
Print Buying Services (03) 565 1666
Print Projects (03) 429 6888
Production Line (03) 427 9292
Stan Matthews (03) 696 0447
Peter Stephenson (03) 614 4600. P 45254.
Wellington House (03) 529 6944. Page 44.

PRINT PRODUCTION CONSULTANTS: WESTERN AUSTRALIA.

Print Hotline (09) 321 4544
Printing Resources (09) 322 3043
Print Marketing Services (09) 364 1149

CREATIVE CONSULTANTS: NEW SOUTH WALES

Adventors (02) 957 3657
Artzell (02) 439 6800
Ausan-Jap Com (02) 953 0300
Aust Bus Theatre (02) 954 0300
Austin, Graham (02) 953 8344
Berry's Creative (02) 909 1211
Brass Tacks (02) 925 0022
Campbell & Me (042) 27 3213
Carson, Gay (02) 957 5567
Charisma Marktg (02) 953 0144
Copywrite Hotshop (02) 957 3877
Corp Story Teller (02) 358 6355
Crawley, Jon (02) 923 1450
Creative Connection (02) 652 2179
Creative Plus (02) 969 8716
Davis, Penny (02) 32 2538
Donger, Tony (02) 957 3877
Dynamic Graphics (02) 949 6244
Espresso Creative (02) 922 3485
Fahey Communications (02) 929 5011
Fergs (02) 957 5107
Ferguson, Peter (02) 969 6571
Genesis (02) 92 4690
Gunn, Robert (02) 922 5566
Heggie, Sabina (02) 929 9547
Hughson Isles (02) 358 1210
Inhaus (02) 631 7100
Invetech (02) 319 2999
Jones & Davis (02) 960 4888
Knowles, Bob (02) 908 4870
Leong, Nelson (02) 332 2933
Lewis, Andrew (02) 959 4800
McCourt, Rory (02) 929 4849
Main Artery (02) 487 2269
Mark Overett Prod (02) 954 0303
Mitchell Art Services (02) 958 5501
Morgan, Guy (02) 909 2130
O'Brien, Richard (02) 922 3622
Omnigraphic (02) 438 1411
Otes, Andy (02) 451 0504
Paddington Wordsmith (02) 331 3978
Passanisi & Assoc (02) 439 4744
Peter Cox Concepts (02) 918 0731
Priday Pty Ltd (02) 949 7219
Pro-notions (02) 906 7219
Quantum Leap (02) 906 3844
Radio Shop (02) 908 1200
Rainbow Graphics (02) 922 3622
Rayner, John (02) 407 3366
Reid, John (02) 398 9751
Richardson, Jenny (02) 439 2694. Page 46.
Ridley, Jim (02) 369 1777
Rogerson, Drewe (02) 261 2144
Schlesinger, A & M (02) 399 6650
Shaw, Gail (02) 360 4179
Silver Bullett (02) 908 3144
Shimmin, Meredith (02) 957 5567
Speaight, Roger (02) 449 5859
Spontaneous Growth (02) 954 9203
Step to the Left (02) 954 4641
SuperVisions (02) 954 0354
Taylor, Martin (02) 487 2269
Theordore, Des (02) 438 1125
TKR Graphics (02) 633 4188
Unique Designs (02) 552 8094
What's the Big Idea (02) 522 8094
Wilson Villani & Assoc (02) 212 3866
Words & Pictures (02) 399 6650
Yes, that's Right (02) 698 9396

CREATIVE CONSULTANTS: QUEENSLAND.

Alwinton, Janine (07) 369 8643
Morrie Brewer (07) 229 1955
Cooper, Elizabeth (07) 221 1905
Goldfinger Enterprises (07) 832 1451
Goodall, Maggie (07) 870 4629
Harris, Vicki (07) 368 2193
Harvoe, Peter (07) 394 2544
Hauritz (07) 395 5031
Hush Creative (07) 832 5729
Imagery Marketing (075) 93 1568
Lightfoot, Peter (07) 369 4561
Lloyd, Carol (07) 839 0100
Macrae, Michael (071) 53 1133
Mullins, Brian (07) 368 1700
Nouveau Image (07) 844 6911
Overett, Mark (07) 368 2688
Revesby Communications (07) 252 2544
Ross Words (07) 378 0916
Sunshine Studios (07) 844 6844
Treacy, John (07) 847 1100

CREATIVE CONSULTANTS: SOUTH AUSTRALIA.

Ad-One Advertising (08) 352 5862
Carless Organisation (08) 271 7131
Dymond, Rosalin (08) 373 0970
Haarsma, Geoff (08) 362 0057
Harris, David (08) 223 5395
Hill, Haydn (08) 272 1300
Hobbs, Shez (08) 231 6679
Holden Edgecombe Holt (08) 272 8855
Honeywill Reid (08) 373 3303
Katron Creative (08) 231 0636
Original Concepts (08) 373 0120
Original Design Co (08) 267 4515
Write Direction (08) 271 2515

CREATIVE CONSULTANTS: VICTORIA.

Ad Infinitum (03) 489 9091
Augustine Greenwood (03) 696 5518
Beanham, Sarah (03) 819 1302
Beatty, Ray (03) 267 3299
Boag, Jeff (03) 818 7817
Canning Communications (03) 696 2499
Carnell, Russell (03) 489 9514
Chadwick, Susan (03) 509 6532
Crichton Creative (52) 83 1253
Christmas Presence (03) 417 2229
Coleman Creative (03) 525 6011
Coombe, Graham (03) 879 0818
Baker Hill (03) 696 5177
Bisetto Patty (03) 417 5592
Bowden, Mick (03) 819 2872
Braley, Ivor (03) 801 5149
Bristow & Prentice (03) 696 6355. Page 64, 65.
Cobalt Blue (03) 696 6810
Communication Works (03) 663 5133
Competitive Edge (03) 429 9000
Coote, Maree (03) 534 4611
Corporate Personality (03) 329 5770
Corporate Story (03) 817 5699. Page 47.
Creative Marketing (03) 817 6461
Dare Concepts (03) 696 3757
Dorneau & Stainsby (03) 646 7652
Drake, Susan (03) 529 6764
Everett & Kamienko (03) 827 4344
Geeves, Tony (03) 699 4911
Gerry Co (03) 531 4765
Graphic Influence (03) 528 2552
Harris, James, Duncan (03) 696 5046
Hauser, Don (03) 654 7610
Hillard, David (03) 241 4344
IMR Marketing (03) 500 9711
James, Roger (03) 846 2920
Kosmedia Com (03) 699 3395
Kuhl & Assoc (03) 481 5357
Labatlus, David (03) 798 6686
M.H. Leffler (03) 419 8777
Little, Craig (03) 596 7268
McGee, Peter (03) 429 8586
Ron, McPhee (03) 523 8133
McTaggart, Elaine (03) 817 5699
Malone, James (03) 439 9474
Markby Conley (03) 646 3633
Marshall, J.R. (03) 525 4534
Merry, J & L (03) 509 5738
More Marketing (03) 699 2611
Morgan Marketing (03) 580 8931
Moss, John (03) 521 1661
Nimble, Sage (03) 696 1366
O'Shea & Assoc (03) 817 2102
Pantelis, Paul (03) 866 3355
Parnham & Assoc (03) 592 6634
Pelman, Amanda (03) 867 7058
Piatowski, Jeff (03) 696 6188
Pittaway Consultancy (03) 820 0433
Ralph, Chris (03) 596 3143
Schmideg, Peter (03) 523 9595
Sheridan, Bob (03) 646 6140
Standish, Conrad (03) 645 2077
Stitt, Alex & Paddy (03) 826 8451. Page 45
Susman, Victor (03) 826 4675
Taylor Text (03) 690 4188
Us (03) 529 2326
Visual Contact (03) 419 9723. Page 48
Webster, David (03) 699 5800
Words at Work (03) 521 1010

CREATIVE CONSULTANTS: WESTERN AUSTRALIA.

Abbey Communications (09) 474 2021
Beynon, Roger (09) 368 2554
Billings, Martin (09) 388 1799
Copy Shop (09) 321 8498
Davis, John (09) 387 8111
Deighton, Mary (09) 399 7283
Goodlet, Ross (09) 368 2560
Hooper Design (09) 344 2323
J & E Copywriting (09) 481 2089
Just Write (09) 322 5516
McAuliffe Creative (09) 381 1206
Scott, Gail (09) 227 6028
Strutt, Jonathan (09) 332 1428

CBD

Corporate Business Design 1

Need an extra copy of this book ?

Phone or Fax Armadillo to check if we have some left.
Send a cheque for $69.95.
or:
Fax a company order, or your Bankcard or Visa number, with its expiry date.
We'll despatch you a copy on receipt, and keep you on our files in order to inform you about future editions.

Armadillo Publishers Pty Ltd,
205-207 Scotchmer Street,
Fitzroy North,
Victoria 3068
Australia.
(03) 489 9559 Fax (03) 489 5576

1

Much more where this came from.

Corporate Business Design follows hot on the trail of Armadillo's other highly successful publication, Creative Source Australia, the Wizards of Oz.

Now in its ninth edition, the Wizards of Oz has sourced a wealth of Australia's top creative talent and shown their work to prospective clients and all buyers of creativity in the advertising, publishing, educational and corporate world. It has a wider scope than this first CBD, encompassing the vital areas of professional photography, illustration, animation and design, plus all ancillary areas such as special effects, model, set and prop construction, styling, food styling, paper sculpture, etc.

If your company doesn't have any editions of the Wizards of Oz, the wise course to take would be to buy the current edition, and if you find it useful, buy a set of back copies.

The total collection encompasses most of the top operators working in Australia today whilst the current edition updates their contact phone number in the Ozwhozu.

If you can't find who or what you're looking for in the current edition, study through the back copies and discover an enormous diversity of ideas and creators.

Fax a copy of the following order form, with your bankcard or visa number, with its expiry date, to Armadillo on (03) 489 5576.

Or send a cheque or company order to us marking which copies you'd like.

ORDER FORM

Please send the following editions of The Wizards of Oz.

☐ copies The Wizards of Oz No. 9 at $85. ☐ copies No. 8 at $85. ☐ copies No. 7 at $80. ☐ copies No. 6 at $70. Total $

☐ copies No. 5 at $60. ☐ copies No. 4 at $55. ☐ copies No. 3 at $48. ☐ copies No. 2 at $39.

Payment by: ☐ Bankcard. ☐ Visa. Card No: Expiry Date:

☐ Endorsed Company order. ☐ Cheque or money order payable to Armadillo Publishers.

Name

Address

Postcode

Armadillo Publishers. 205-207 Scotchmer St, Fitzroy North Vic 3068 Australia.
(03) 489 9559 Fax (03) 489 5576.

Armadillo Publishers Pty Ltd.
205-207 Scotchmer Street, Fitzroy North,
Victoria 3068. Australia. (03) 489 9559.

ARE YOU LISTED?

For 10 years now, Armadillo Publishers has been compiling and updating its file of creative personnel.

With CBD, we are expanding into a slightly different area and initially some people who feel they should be within our pages, may not be.

Don't just sit and moan, send us your business card or better still, a short precis of your services. This will ensure we know all about you and will then continue to keep you up to date with our forthcoming publications.

If we have you on our files, you will then be listed in one of the creative categories in either the CBD or its companion publication, Creative Source Australia, the Wizards of Oz.

Unlike some publications, we do not publish addresses from our lists as we believe it's an intrusion of privacy.

We list names or Company names and phone numbers, and eventually fax numbers.

However, for our files, we require a name, company name, address, phone and fax number.

Armadillo Publishers Pty Ltd.
205-207 Scotchmer Street, Fitzroy North. Victoria 3068
Phone (03) 489 9559. Fax (03) 489 5576